ONE FOR THE
AGELESS

HOW TO STAY YOUNG AND IMMATURE
EVEN IF YOU'RE REALLY OLD

JERRY ZEZIMA

ONE FOR THE AGELESS
HOW TO STAY YOUNG AND IMMATURE
EVEN IF YOU'RE REALLY OLD

iUniverse books may be ordered through booksellers or by contacting:

iUniverse
1663 Liberty Drive
Bloomington, IN 47403
www.iuniverse.com
844-349-9409

ISBN: 978-1-6632-3550-3 (sc)
ISBN: 978-1-6632-3551-0 (e)

Print information available on the last page.

iUniverse rev. date: 01/31/2022

ALSO BY JERRY ZEZIMA

"Leave It to Boomer: A Look at Life, Love and Parenthood by the Very Model of the Modern Middle-Age Man"

"The Empty Nest Chronicles: How to Have Fun (and Stop Annoying Your Spouse) After the Kids Move Out"

"Grandfather Knows Best: A Geezer's Guide to Life, Immaturity, and Learning How to Change Diapers All Over Again"

"Nini and Poppie's Excellent Adventures: Grandkids, Wine Clubs, and Other Ways to Keep Having Fun"

"Every Day Is Saturday: Sleeping Late, Playing With the Grandchildren, Surviving the Quarantine, and Other Joys of Retirement"

PRAISE FOR JERRY ZEZIMA

"That Jerry Zezima is one funny guy! Or maybe two. Who knows? I've never actually seen him in person."

— *Brian Crane, Reuben Award-winning cartoonist and creator of the syndicated comic strip "Pickles"*

"As an aging boomer, humorist Jerry Zezima has seen it all. And he still does, although now he squints. His columns remain a joy of insights, his humor fresh, and his grandchildren adorable. From his observations on rules of the road for shopping carts to his hammock war with mice, Jerry proves that one can grow old gracefully and with great humor, while maturing not at all."

— *Dave Jaffe, author of "Sleeping Between Giants: Life, If You Can Call It That, With a Terrier"*

"Only read this book if you like to laugh! Jerry Zezima's latest, 'One for the Ageless: How to Stay Young and Immature Even If You're Really Old,' is the right medicine for the pandemic blues. His stories are laugh-out-loud funny (so you should not read this in a library or with a full bladder). And at the same time, you will find yourself choked up by the sweetness of his experiences as a grandparent. For that, thank goodness, there is no cure. Enjoy!"

— *Kathy Eliscu, author of "Not Even Dark Chocolate Can Fix This Mess"*

"Jerry Zezima's warm, zany accounts of life make getting creaky and cranky actually seem like good fun. His 'Supermarket Driving Test' is a work of genius. However, if your carcass only hurts when you chortle, you probably should consult a physician before perusing this collection."

— *John Rolfe, columnist, humorist, blogger at Celestial Chuckle, and author of "The Goose in the Bathroom: Stirring Tales of Family Life"*

"Jerry Zezima — ageless to his core — has done it again with his new book, which is chock full of humor, poignancy, and grace. For Jerry, age is just a state of mind. And what a mind he has, reminding us with each gifted chapter that an 'immature geezer' can remain a child at heart. Jerry will make you laugh and cry, and will prove that growing up has little to do with growing old, and that if you do it right, you can stay young forever. Another gem of a read as only Jerry Zezima, the master of wit and wisdom, can do it."

— *Judith Marks-White, author of "Seducing Harry" and "Bachelor Degree"*

"Few writers can tell personal stories that are as touching and relatable as they are laugh-out-loud funny, but with 'One for the Ageless,' Jerry Zezima again proves that he belongs in that small but talented club. Mining his relatively normal American life for moments of essential truth and hysterical comedy, Jerry finds the gold that glows with both, making our own lives feel brighter and more connected. A must-read for anyone who, like Jerry, values living, learning, and laughing — not necessarily in that order."

— *Joel Schwartzberg, author of "Get to the Point!"*
and "The Language of Leadership"

"Zezima's latest anecdotes about life in retirement pack colossal humor into bite-sized stories, revealing a man unfalteringly devoted to his wife and family."

— *From BookLife (Editor's Pick) review of "Every Day Is Saturday"*

"[Zezima's] work is filled with chuckles … His upbeat take on aspects of everyday life offers pleasant distraction from today's stresses."

— *From Kirkus Reviews*

CONTENTS

DEDICATION

To Sue, with whom I love growing old — and staying young.

ACKNOWLEDGMENTS

To my family, whose immediate members don't seem bothered by the fact that I have lasted this long, despite having to put up with a daily torrent of my stupid jokes.

To Katie Foran-McHale, Zach Finken, and Aaron Gilman, my wonderful editors at Tribune News Service, which is unwittingly contributing to the decline of the newspaper industry by distributing my column to papers nationwide and abroad.

To Brian Crane, Dave Jaffe, Kathy Eliscu, John Rolfe, Judith Marks-White, and Joel Schwartzberg, not only for writing glowing blurbs for this book, but for admitting they even know me.

And to Marty Cain, Ellie Go, Christine Colborne, and all the other good folks at iUniverse for publishing this book, my sixth for the house. May you never learn your lesson.

INTRODUCTION

Age, goes an old (of course) saying, is just a number. As a geezer who flunked math in school and now has the checkbook to prove it, I believe this adage for a number of reasons. I'm not sure how many because I am, you know, bad at math.

At any rate, the whole thing dawned on me, even though it wasn't dawn, when my daughter Katie turned forty.

When I reached that age, twenty-eight (thank you, calculator!) years ago, I was reminded of another adage: Life begins at forty.

If that's true, I realized, I had just wasted thirty-nine years.

I also realized that milestones are like kidney stones: They're hard to pass, but at least after you pass a kidney stone, you feel better.

Still, reaching birthdays ending in zero has never bothered me. That's because I am a baby boomer, a member of the generation that used to say, "Don't trust anyone over thirty." Now that most of us are at least twice that age, we have developed a mathematical formula that would have earned us failing grades in school.

Here it is: Sixty is the new fifty. Or, even better, sixty is the new forty.

I don't know if this makes Katie feel better (I doubt it), but it does wonders for me — except for one thing:

If I insisted I was forty, not only would I be the same age as my daughter, which would entail flunking both biology and algebra, but I'd have to come out of retirement and go back to work. Even I'm not that stupid.

To any baby boomer who worries about those accumulating birthdays, I would tell you that this is the best time of life. Not only can you still do everything you have always done, but if there is something you don't want to do, you can pull the age card.

"I don't think I should be lugging furniture anymore," you might say to anyone who is younger, which these days includes almost everyone.

"I don't think I should be shoveling snow anymore," you might say to no one in particular, because no one in particular will listen to you.

What you should say is: "I do think I should be lying in a hammock with a beer."

This seldom works on spouses who not only are the same age but have a whole list of chores, errands, and household projects for you to do.

There are two ways around this:

(a) Misplace the list. "I'm old," you can then say. "What did you expect?"

(b) Do the chores so badly ("You mean I can't use toilet bowl cleaner to wash the dishes?") that you will never be asked to do them again.

The most difficult part about getting older is putting up with birthday candle jokes. Like:

"What are you going to light them with, a flamethrower?"

"You'll have to call the fire department to put them all out!"

"What's the difference between you and your birthday cake? You're not so hot anymore."

I can't say that about my wife, Sue, who is my age but looks years younger and, yes, is still hot. We have been married for forty-four years. Without her, I would be either dead or in prison.

You will read a lot about Sue in this book. You'll also read about Katie and her younger sister, Lauren; about Katie and Lauren's husbands, Dave and Guillaume; and about the grandkids: Chloe and Lilly, who are Lauren and Guillaume's daughters, and Xavier, Zoe, and Quinn, who are Katie and Dave's children. The kids range in age from nine to almost three. And they're all more mature than I am.

Because of the pandemic, Sue and I didn't see Chloe and Lilly in person for months. And on the rare occasions when we could get together, it was outside, often in the cold, while masked and at a safe social distance, meaning we couldn't hug, kiss, or — in my case — act silly with them. Even worse, we hadn't seen Xavier, Zoe, and Quinn in person for a year and a half. We missed a lot. Thank goodness for FaceTime.

Now that restrictions have been lifted, we've been having family reunions, which you'll also read about.

This book contains plenty of other real-life characters, the vast majority of whom are, naturally, younger than I am.

The notable exception is my mother, Rosina, who is ninety-seven and is sharper than I am. I admit that this isn't such a great accomplishment because the same could be said for cucumbers. But my mom has grown old gracefully, as well as gratefully, with a positive outlook and a fabulous sense of humor.

I wouldn't be surprised if she reaches one hundred. We will, of course, invite the fire department to the birthday party.

CHAPTER 1

(Growing old together is a wonderful concept — until both spouses are retired. It can still be wonderful, although adding shampoo to the shopping list can't prevent the aging lovebirds from getting in each other's hair.)

"The Spouse In the House"

After I retired, which raised the question of how I could stop working when I never really started, I realized that I still had two jobs: babysitting my grandchildren and driving my wife crazy.

The first was easy because the kids ended up babysitting me.

The second was difficult because Sue was still working, so she wasn't around every day for me to tell her stupid jokes, follow her around like a puppy, and generally, though absolutely without question, make her want to scream.

Now that she has retired, it's a lot easier to get that reaction from her.

When I offered, on one of the first days of her retirement, to go to the supermarket for her, which would have entailed calling home every three minutes to ask where each item on her shopping list was, Sue said, "You stay here and I'll go to the store. I have to get out of the house."

Such is the situation when an otherwise loving couple find themselves together 24/7.

Sue had been a teacher's assistant for three decades. Working with children is the highest calling. It's the world's most important job — except, of course, for being my doctor.

When the pandemic hit, Sue started working remotely, which meant she didn't have to get up at five-thirty every weekday morning. She could sleep later, do a minimal amount of work, and have the rest of the day to spend with me.

It gave her a good idea of what she had to look forward to.

"Is this what retirement is going to be like?" she moaned on more than one occasion, usually after I had just made some typically inane remark.

"Yes!" I chirped. "Isn't it great?"

Since Sue's retirement became official, we have found plenty of fun things to do together.

Like applying for Medicare Part B.

"This is enough to give you a headache," Sue said.

"Is aspirin covered?" I asked.

"Forget aspirin," Sue said. "How about wine?"

Then there's the joy of trying to get supplemental insurance.

"You know what the best plan is?" Sue said after one of many frustrating phone calls.

"What?" I replied.

"The one I had at work," she said. "Now I don't have a job."

Unlike me, Sue doesn't still have two jobs: Because of the quarantine, she can't babysit our grandchildren and, because I'm already of unsound mind, she can't drive me crazy.

What she can do is enjoy her newfound freedom. She loves to go for walks and ride her bike. Even more, she loves sleeping in and letting me get up first to make the coffee.

"I'm thinking of taking up knitting," she said one morning.

"Maybe I should, too," I told her. "I'll have you in stitches."

Sue rolled her eyes. I rolled them back and poured each of us a cup of java.

"Have I driven you bonkers?" I asked.

"Not yet," Sue said as she took a sip.

"Good," I replied. "This is what retirement is all about. In fact, you'll be crazy about it."

"They Don't Have Me Covered"

When it comes to being stuck, there is nothing stronger than red tape. I should know because I had to unravel an entire roll of the stuff in a maddening effort to get a Medicare Part B card.

According to Social Security, through which I had to apply, causing me insecurity, Part B covers physician services, outpatient hospital services, certain home health services, durable medical equipment, and certain other medical and health services not covered by Part A.

Naturally, there is a hefty cover charge even though you still need supplemental insurance for things not covered by Part B.

I applied after Sue retired. Her insurance at work covered me until she didn't work anymore and left me uncovered, something you don't want to happen if the weather is chilly or there are cops around.

Sue got her Part B card right away. My card, which I figured was the seven of clubs, never came.

So I called Social Security and spoke with a friendly guy named Todd.

"Part B or not Part B — that is the question," I said after being on hold for a period longer than the Super Bowl halftime show.

"I hate to say this," he said, and proceeded to say it anyway, "but it's the government."

"My tax dollars at work," I said. "Or maybe my tax dollars don't work and are retired, like me."

"It sounds stupid," Todd acknowledged, "but that's red tape for you."

"Don't you have any green or blue tape?" I wondered.

"No, it's always red," said Todd, adding: "You were about to get a denial letter."

"Then I would have been in denial," I responded.

"It's a good thing you called," Todd said.

"When was I supposed to find this out?" I asked.

"When you called," replied Todd, noting that I would need another 564 form, which would require a 561 form and two 40B forms.

"This is a pain in the neck," I said, though I actually referred to a lower anatomical region. "Would it be covered?"

"I don't know if chiropractors are on the list," replied Todd, who said he'd be happy to help me get the whole mess straightened out.

"I already have Medicare Part A," I said.

"I handle A and B," said Todd, "but there's also C, which is supplemental, and D, for drugs."

"Can I use the drugs to get rid of my headache?" I asked.

"Yes," Todd answered, adding that there also are Parts E, F, and G.

"Do I have to go through the entire alphabet?" I wanted to know.

"You might," said Todd, who's thirty-seven and nowhere near retirement. "If I didn't work here," he admitted, saying he had trained for months, "I'd be totally lost, too."

Todd also admitted that his nine-year-old son is more tech-savvy than he is.

"He has his own iPad," Todd said.

"I don't have an iPad or an iPod," I said, "but I do have iTeeth. Would they be covered under the dental plan?"

"I hope so," said Todd, who got me processed and promised that my Part B card would soon be delivered.

"Just to make sure it arrives," I said, "don't seal the envelope with red tape."

"A Coffee Maker's Brew Haha"

I have reached the age (old enough to know better) where getting a good night's sleep depletes me so much, especially if I dream about something exciting, like sleeping, that I need a liquid boost to start the day.

No, silly, not gin. I mean coffee.

And it's my dumb luck to make it better than Sue, which is why, on most mornings, I have to get up first to brew a pot of rich, dark, steaming hot java that gets the blood circulating and puts smiles on our faces, at least until the caffeine wears off.

Often I will detect, after getting up quietly to use the porcelain convenience, that Sue is awake on her side of the bed, pretending to be asleep so I will stay up and make the coffee.

Down the stairs I thump, yawning and stretching, attorneys-at-law, and stumble into the kitchen, where I put a filter into the basket of the coffee maker and begin the meticulous process of measuring the exact amount of ground beans: seven even scoops, one bulging scoop, and — this is the key — a pinch that would barely cover an ant, which you definitely don't want in your kitchen, and especially in your coffee.

Then I fill the pot with faucet-fed water, flick the switch, and — voila! — realize I haven't plugged in the machine. Once I do, the percolation commences.

Ten minutes later, five beeps indicate that the coffee is done, at which time Sue enters the kitchen. I pour her a large cup of coffee and put in a splash of milk. She takes a sip, smiles, and says, "Good! You make it better than I do."

She's right. I have had Sue's coffee. It's not so strong that it will take the paint off the wall (I'm off the wall, so I should know) or so weak that it will fail to awaken the aforementioned ant.

It's just, well, not as good as mine.

Such is the curse of the man who never used to drink coffee. In fact, I had always considered coffee a stupid drink. It's made from beans that are grown on mountains and brought down by mules so they can be ground into grounds, through which hot water is run.

I prefer a sensible drink. Like beer.

I once brewed my own brew, which I called Jerry's Nasty Ale. Actually, it wasn't bad. It had an inadvertently smoky taste, which I couldn't figure out since I didn't put cigar ashes in it, and earned raves from Sue and a couple of neighbors, who did not, thank God, have to be hospitalized.

Another sensible drink is wine, which I have also made. The first time, I got grapes from a vineyard, brought them home, stomped on them with my bare feet like Lucille Ball did in "I Love Lucy," bottled the concoction, let it ferment for a couple of weeks, and brought it back to the vineyard, where the winemaker tried it and exclaimed, "It tastes like nail polish remover!"

I went back the following year to help him make the real thing, mainly by shoveling grape skins out of a vat and watching him do the rest. The resultant vintage was wonderful.

But it wasn't nearly as good as my coffee.

"Delicious!" Sue said this morning after taking her first sip.

"I'm glad," I replied, waiting for the caffeine to kick in, "that you don't have grounds for complaint."

"Hot Stuff in the Kitchen"

I'm the very model of the modern modest man. That is why I am somewhat reluctant but still kind of excited to announce that there is a sex scandal going on in my house.

And it involves, of all things, Tupperware.

This is hot news for two reasons:

(a) Now that Thanksgiving is over, and I am more stuffed than the turkey, it is time to use the plastic containers for leftovers, which is what I will be eating until Christmas, after which I will be eating leftovers until Valentine's Day, after which I will explode like the Hindenburg. Oh, the calamity!

(b) Tupperware profits are even more prodigious these days than leftovers.

According to a story by The Associated Press, "Restaurant pain has turned into Tupperware's gain with millions of people in a pandemic opening cookbooks again and looking for solutions to leftovers. They've found it again in Tupperware, suddenly an 'it brand' five decades after what seemed to be its glory days."

I hate to say this, but Tupperware is also having glory nights in my house. This explains why it seems to be reproducing at an alarming rate in one of the kitchen cabinets, where topless containers must be having midnight orgies. Then they give birth to baby containers that must be burped.

I can't open the cabinet door without being pelted by a torrent of Tupperware. It's a good thing we don't keep crockery up there. Or bowling balls.

An inventory revealed these startling figures: fifty-three containers but only forty-nine tops. There are an additional seven containers and three tops in the garage, where the excess Tupperware is kept because the cabinet is jammed with the stuff.

Then there is the refrigerator census. There are five containers with leftovers: pork chops, eggplant, meatloaf, scallion patties, and pork lo mein.

Tupperware total: sixty-five containers and fifty-seven tops.

Not all of it is technically Tupperware, but it's plastic nonetheless, some from the Chinese restaurant down the street, some from a discount store, some from the supermarket, and some, presumably, from a midnight invasion by inanimate objects that heard of the nasty shenanigans and wanted to get in on the action.

I often feel like Dustin Hoffman in "The Graduate," where a slimy guy sidles up to him and says, "Plastics. ... There's a great future in plastics. Think about it."

I've thought about it, especially at night, when I can't get to sleep because I'm wondering what the hell is going on in the kitchen cabinet.

If the population explosion continues, we'll be able to store enough leftovers to feed New Zealand.

Sue, the Empress of Tupperware, did use a container for what I thought was a noble purpose: She kept leftover wine in it. This became necessary because we are the kind of sophisticated people who buy wine in boxes. When I poured a wee too much but couldn't put it back in the box (never a problem when you buy bottles or simply down the rest of the wine and have to go to bed), Sue poured it in a Tupperware container.

I had the leftover wine the next night. It had a piquant plastic aftertaste that tickled the palate!

I needed fortification when contemplating the mathematical dilemma of having an unequal amount of containers and tops. Or, after an exhaustive search, finding the right container for whatever meal you couldn't finish but not the corresponding top.

This is another mean trick that Tupperware plays during the night: The containers and tops purposely separate in the cabinet so you have to go through them all before finding the mates. Sometimes it takes so long that the food spoils before it can be refrigerated.

Now we are faced with Thanksgiving leftovers. At least we have enough Tupperware.

"Banks for Nothing, Moneybags"

If I ever won Powerball and survived the shock, a technical necessity since you can't collect if you are legally dead, I still wouldn't be in the money. That's because Sue, a neat person, would inadvertently throw out the ticket or I, a messy person, would put the ticket somewhere in the house for safekeeping and never find it again.

But I am happy to report that my heart is still beating, albeit at a much faster rate, because I have just won one million euros in the Spanish Lotto Lottery and am eligible to win $1.3 billion in the year-end drawing of the Euro Millo Lottery.

The timing couldn't have been better because approximately half an hour before receiving the good news via email, it took my bank exactly three seconds to reject my online application for a line of credit.

Stunned at the speed with which I was rejected, which was even faster than what I experienced on the dating scene before I met Sue, I called the bank's 800 number and was connected to the "fulfillment department."

After hearing a disembodied voice say that the call "may be monitored and/or recorded for quality assurance purposes," I spoke with a "customer service specialist" named Tesshana.

"There is some delinquency on your credit," she said.

"I used to be a juvenile delinquent," I told her. "I'm all grown up now, but I'm still juvenile. Will you give me credit for that?"

"I'm afraid I can't," said Tesshana.

"The bank must have set the world record for fastest rejection," I noted.

"It doesn't take long at all," Tesshana explained. "Thank you for being a valued client and have a good day."

The rejection caused dejection until I got an email from Paul Schmiitz, award consulting director of the Spanish Lotto Lottery, informing me of my fabulous winnings.

I phoned him but got this recording: "Your call cannot be completed as dialed. Please check the number and call again."

So I sent him the following email:

Dear Mr. Schmiitz:

I'm Jerry Zezima, an internationally syndicated newspaper columnist whose work, I am proud to say, has no redeeming social value.

Because I had to take a vow of poverty when I went into journalism, and because I was just rejected for a bank loan, and because the price of beer has gone up during the pandemic, I was beside myself (my wife was in another room) with excitement to receive your email informing me that I have won one million euros in the Spanish Lotto Lottery.

If that weren't generous enough (the mortgage is due, so it isn't), I am eligible to participate in the Euro Millo Lottery's year-end drawing for $1.3 billion. That's a lot of beer money. I'm not sure I would take it all in one lump's sum because it would only weigh down my pants and put me in a higher tax bracket.

Still, I am so excited about this windfall that I would like to write a column about you and the lottery. As proof of just how low journalistic standards have sunk, my column runs in papers around the world, so you would be getting lots of free publicity. After giving me all that money, it's probably the only kind you could afford.

Thanks very much, Mr. Schmiitz. I await your reply (and the one million euros) with bated breath. In the meantime, I guess I should brush my teeth.

Sincerely,
Jerry Zezima

P.S. Pay the phone bill. Your number is out of service.

I am shocked to say that I have not heard back. But the bank and the lottery can keep the money. As long as I have enough for beer, I'll consider myself a rich man.

"You Don't Have to Pardon My French"

I have long considered myself a Francophile, which is defined as someone who loves ballpark franks, because my son-in-law Guillaume is from France.

9

So it was only natural that I decided, during a car (voiture) ride with Guillaume, who was on a hands-free phone call with his mother (mère) and father (père) while I ate a bag of French (français) fries, to learn French (ditto).

Guillaume has been teaching Chloe, his seven-year-old daughter (fille) and my granddaughter (petite fille), the beautiful language (langue) of his homeland.

This is being done with an app called Duolingo. It features Duo, a little green owl (chouette vert) who helps monolingual (I am not even going to look it up) people such as me (moi) learn French, Spanish, and many other languages, including the most wonderful of all: Pig Latin.

Guillaume downloaded Duolingo on my cellphone, which also has apps for the weather (météo), the news (actualités), a calculator (calculatrice), a camera (caméra), and my bank account (empty).

I started by answering several questions, the first being: "Why are you learning a language?"

The answers included: family and friends, culture, brain training, school, job opportunities, and travel.

Because I get my culture from yogurt, I don't have a brain, I don't go to school, I don't want a job, and I can't travel, I chose family and friends, even though, for what must be obvious reasons, I don't have too many of the latter.

Then I had to pick one of four goals: casual (five minutes a day), regular (ten minutes), serious (fifteen), and intense (twenty).

"Pick casual," Guillaume suggested. "You should start slow."

"Merci," I said, thanking him in French, before adding: "I've always been slow, even in English."

But I got off to a fast (rapide) start when I was given questions such as: "How do you say croissant?"

The choices were: le garçon, le homme, le chat, and le croissant.

I hesitated a minute (une minute), figuring it was a trick question, before answering: "Le croissant."

A musical flourish — ta-da! (French translation: ta-da!) — burst from the phone.

"Amazing!" it said under my correct answer.

After correctly answering several other easy (facile) questions, I finished the day's lesson with a perfect (parfait) score.

"Great job!" it said on the screen. "You reached your daily goal! Lesson complete!"

Duo himself popped up and, with his tiny wings (ailes), applauded me. I felt like a million euros.

I felt even better (meilleur) the next day, when I breezed through Lesson 2 (deux), translating such sentences as: "Je suis un chat." ("I am a cat.")

This meant, of course, that I was the chat's meow.

On the third (troisième) day, I was asked this question: "Tu es un cheval?" ("Are you a horse?") I was glad that after horse, it didn't say "derrière."

The next day I was informed that "thirty-four hours on Duolingo teaches you as much as one semester at a university."

I hadn't learned enough French to ask if I would go bankrupt paying tuition. Fortunately, the app is free (gratuit).

The last day was so easy — at one point I was shown pictures of an orange, a croissant, and a pizza and was asked to identify the pizza — that I would have tipped my hat to myself, except I don't own a beret (béret).

When I told Guillaume I did well in my first week, he said, "Yes."

"You mean oui," I corrected him.

When I spoke with Chloe, she was even more impressed.

"Très bien (very good), Poppie!" she said.

In looking back on a memorable (mémorable) week, I can truly say that, at least on my cellphone, I'll always have Paris.

"Wackos Create an Identity Crisis"

One of Sammy Davis Jr.'s best and most popular songs was "I've Gotta Be Me." Even though I can't sing, it should be my theme song because nobody else wants to be me. That's why my identity has never been stolen.

I can't say the same for Sue, who noticed suspicious activity on one of her credit cards, received a mysterious box containing junk she'd never ordered, and had to go to the bank to straighten the whole mess out.

I accompanied her to see what it was like to be wanted by somebody other than the police.

The drama, sponsored by a company named for a river in South America (sorry, you're wrong, it's not the Orinoco), began when Sue saw a charge for $54.28.

"Did you buy something?" she asked me.

I professed my innocence and said, "I wouldn't know how."

A few days later, a prompt parcel person plopped a package on our doorstep, made a beeline back to his truck, and sped away.

Sue took the box inside and saw that her name had been misspelled.

"How could anyone misspell 'Sue'?" I wondered.

"No," she said with a sigh. "I mean the last name."

It was spelled "Zezmimia."

"Sounds like a small country or some kind of unpleasant ointment," I said. "Either way, I couldn't spell the name until I was in high school."

Sue tore open the box and discovered the contents: a fake spider's web, five wishing lights, and an insulated lunch bag.

"If someone's going to send stuff," Sue huffed, "they could have ordered something good."

That prompted a call to the aforementioned company and a conversation with a very nice customer service specialist named Chanel.

"This is what they do," she said, referring to the fraudsters who attempt to steal the identities of law-abiding citizens and, it should be noted, online shoppers like Sue. "They'll send a package to your house using your credit card information and then take the package back before you have a chance to bring it in."

"You were too fast for them," I told Sue.

"Speaking of fast," said Chanel, who cleared the charge at her company, "you should go to the bank and get a new card."

Before you could say "Chapter 11," Sue and I were sitting with a helpful financial solutions adviser named Daniel.

"I'm going to freeze the card," he said after taking it from Sue.

"It's safer than incinerating it," I said. "You might burn the bank down."

Daniel politely ignored the remark and said, "It's disconcerting, to say the least."

"If not less," I added.

Daniel called the fraud department and spoke with a claims specialist named Max, who then spoke with Sue.

"He canceled the card," she said after hanging up.

"I guess it was Maxed out," I commented.

"I hate when this happens," Daniel said, presumably referring to identity theft, though he could have been talking about my stupid jokes.

"Nobody wants my identity," I told him.

"I can relate," Daniel said. "I have yet to find a person who wants mine. I'm working on it."

He looked at the computer screen and noted that Sue and I have joint banking.

"It's so we can afford to stay in our joint," I explained. "But after this, if I tried to get into Sue's account, would I be arrested?"

"Yes," said Daniel. "The cops would take both of us out in handcuffs."

After telling Sue that she'd soon be getting a new card, Daniel warned us about credit thievery.

"It's happened to me," he said. "There are a bunch of wacko ding dongs out there."

"That means I'm safe," I said.

"How so?" Daniel asked.

"I'm a wacko ding dong," I answered. "That's why nobody wants my identity."

"Clothes Encounters of the Worst Kind"

If it's true that clothes make the man, which in my case is far more likely than the man making clothes, because I can't sew and would have to go around in my birthday suit, risking either pneumonia or arrest, then I definitely have a fashion plate in my head.

Still, I have to wear something, even if, as a retiree, I don't have to dress for success anymore. Not that I had much success when I was working, but at least now I can lounge around the house in sweatshirts and sweatpants (in fall and winter) or T-shirts and shorts (in spring and summer).

To steal a lyric from the Byrds, there is a season (turn, turn, turn). No, I don't know what the hell it means, either, but I do know that, according to Sue, who is very stylish, I should change my seasonal wardrobe twice a year, putting my summer clothes away and taking out my winter clothes when the weather gets cold and putting my winter clothes away and taking out my summer clothes when the weather gets hot.

And, of course, vice versa.

I never used to do this because I worked in an office where the temperature fluctuated wildly, leading to the terrible realization that there is no such thing as climate control. It got so bad that I once tried to have the National Weather Service declare my desk the coldest spot in the United States.

And this was in the summer. So why put away my winter clothes?

Another reason I have never made the seasonal switch is that my entire wardrobe is made of approximately eight yards of material.

This explains why it is contained to one small closet and three bureau drawers. On the other hand, which requires a glove, Sue has a wardrobe large enough to clothe Luxembourg.

I don't mind because: (a) she looks beautiful in anything she wears, even sweatshirts and sweatpants, since she's now retired, too, and (b) she buys my clothes, thus saving me the horror of having to get dressed up to go shopping.

This year, however, it has been suggested that because I am no longer working, I should put away my summer clothes.

I said to Sue, the person who suggested this bold move, "With global warming, why bother?"

But even I have to concede that it's worth the trouble, if only to get a large plastic bin full of clothes out of my already cluttered office and into the attic, a large space as empty as my skull.

Sue pulled out another bin of clothes from the closet in my office.

"Whose are those?" I asked innocently.

"Yours!" she responded sharply. "You didn't even know they were here."

And there is a pile of unboxed and unfolded clothes on the shelf in my bedroom closet, stuff I have ignored for God knows how long, including ties, which I have seldom worn because they cut off the air supply to my brain; swim trunks, which I should keep in the trunk of my car for when I go swimming; and a pair of paper pants I had to wear several years ago when I got an X-ray for a kidney stone.

So I am now in the process of finally making the seasonal wardrobe switch. I might even find that some of my duds are so old and unstylish, like the guy who owns them, that they can be given away, thrown out, or, if I break out the fire pit, burned.

Still, sadly, no matter what the season, clothes make this man look like a dweeb.

"For Whom the Bell Doesn't Toll"

My greatest fear as a homeowner, aside from undertaking a do-it-yourself plumbing project and being swept away in the resulting flood, is being arrested at gunpoint for breaking into my own house.

I found out that I could have ended up in the penitentiary after talking with an alarm company technician who nearly had the same thing happen to him.

"I once set off a panic alarm in a house where I was working," said Tim Seibert, who was working at my house. "It was a silent holdup. I went outside and there were two cops with guns. I said, 'Don't shoot me, I'm only the alarm guy.' I had to show them proof."

"If that happened to me," I said, "it would be because I locked myself out. And I wouldn't have proof that it was my house."

"You'd end up in jail," said Tim, who had come over because the company ran a test on the alarm system and found that, unbeknownst to me and Sue, it hadn't been working for a month and a half.

"If someone broke in — like you, for instance — the alarm would have gone off in the house, but it wouldn't have registered in the control center, so we wouldn't have known something was wrong," Tim explained.

"So burglars could have made off with all our valuables?" I asked.

"That's right," Tim answered.

"The bad news is that we had no idea we weren't protected," I said. "The good news is that we don't have too many valuables."

It was news to me that, according to Tim, the phone company was to blame. After he inquired about our landline and I told him that we'd had trouble with it and that someone had come over and supposedly fixed it, Tim said, "I see this all the time. They unplug stuff and don't even tell you they did that. It disconnects the alarm and you don't know it."

When Tim reconnected the alarm, it screeched at a decibel level that almost blew out the windows. He jumped. I nearly lost kidney function.

Tim pressed some buttons on the keypad and the screeching mercifully stopped.

"There," he said with a sigh of relief. "You're all set."

When I told Tim that the phone was still acting up, he fixed that, too. But just to make sure, he called my cellphone from the landline. We stood five feet apart. The conversation went like this:

Me: "Hello?"

Tim: "Hi, Jerry."

Me: "Tim?"

Tim: "Yes. Does the phone work?"

Me: "What?"

Tim: "Does the phone work?"

Me: "Who is this?"

Tim hung up and said, "It works."

"You're really handy," I told him.

"I like to solve problems," said Tim.

"I like to cause problems," I noted.

"You could keep me employed," Tim said. "It's like the old saying — job security for guys who don't know what they're doing."

Tim, who's fifty-three and has been in the alarm business for thirty-three years, said his first job was as a bill collector.

"I hated it," he said, adding that he used to repossess cars. "One guy came out yelling. Shortly after that, I quit. But I've had my share of crazy customers in this job, too. Like the guy who kept a gun under his bathroom rug."

After determining that he's made more than fifty thousand service calls, Tim said, "I looked on my log and saw that I was here seven years ago. I knew your name rang a bell."

"A bell?" I said. "Good one!"

Tim smiled and said, "Your house is safe. You don't have to worry about being arrested."

"Thanks," I said. "Now I can tell my wife there's no cause for alarm."

"Diary of a Powerless Homeowner"

Since I am always in the dark, mainly because I'm lightheaded, the recent storm didn't throw shade at me. But it left my house in the dark, too. For six days. So I got a pen and a flashlight and kept a diary because, unfortunately, I was powerless to do anything else.

Tuesday: Tropical Storm Isaias breezes in and knocks out the electricity at 12:30 p.m.

"How could the power go out?" I ask Sue. "It's just drizzling."

The power comes back on at 2 p.m.

"What a wimp of a storm," I say.

Isaias must have heard me because half an hour later he blows through with a vengeance and knocks out the power again.

The storm leaves twigs and branches all over our property. Sue and I go outside after dinner (chicken salad — yum!) to clean up the front yard and see Corrie, our next-door neighbor, who says the power isn't supposed to come back on until Thursday.

I call the power company but can't get through.

"They must be out, too," I chortle.

Darkness descends. I light candles and nearly burn off my fingertips. My phone is almost out of juice, so I get in my air-conditioned (thank God!) car and drive around while charging it. When I arrive back home, it feels like a sauna.

"Let's wear towels!" I tell Sue.

She frowns. I grab a flashlight and try to read a book. It's one of mine. I get drowsy.

We go to bed but can't sleep. Sue gets up and goes into another room, possibly because I forgot to brush my teeth. I'll do it in the morning.

Wednesday: I finally get through to the power company. A recording tells me there is no information about our outage but that crews are "working hard" to restore electricity, which should be back up by Friday.

I wonder how many times I can flick the bathroom light switch before remembering that we have no power.

I spend the entire day cleaning the backyard. I smell to the high heavens. So does some of our food, which Sue throws out.

Thursday: I finally take a shower. The water is so cold it could induce cardiac arrest in a walrus.

Power update: It should be back up by Saturday. I drive around after dark to charge my phone again and notice that every house in the neighborhood but ours and a few others is illuminated like Times Square on New Year's Eve.

Friday: Sue and I drive to the home of Lauren and Guillaume, who have power. Chloe and Lilly are happy we are staying over.

Sue and I sleep in the air-conditioned living room on an air mattress that Lauren's friend Tara kindly lets us use. It's the best rest we've had all week.

Saturday: I play with the girls outside, first on the swings, then in their inflatable pool. Afterward, I have a beer that, unlike the brew in our house, is actually cold.

Power update: They're shooting for Sunday. I'd like to shoot them.

Sunday: Sue and I thank Lauren and Guillaume for their hospitality and drive home. We arrive at 2:45 p.m. and find that there's still no electricity. As Sue throws out the rest of the food, I call the power company and speak with Patti, who apologizes and says, "There are no words."

"There are plenty of words," I tell her. "But I can't repeat them over the phone."

Then, at 6:09 p.m., the house alarm starts blaring.

"We have power!" I squeal.

"Finally!" Sue exults.

I flick the bathroom switch. The light goes on. I'm not in the dark after all.

CHAPTER 2

(The great outdoors aren't so great when weary oldsters have to deal with Mother Nature and her many spiteful critters and damaging storms. Even a day at the beach isn't a day at the beach.)

"Out on a Limb With Yard Work"

Ask any robin, blue jay, or birdbrained homeowner and they will tell you that everything happens in trees.

I know this, and not because a little bird told me, after seeing the debris that several trees left in my yard. Actually, two yards, front and back, which were littered with leaves, twigs, and branches when a storm blew through and knocked out our power for six days.

My power, never in great supply, was knocked out over the course of three days, when I founded Jerry's Landscaping, Tree Trimming & Myocardial Infarction Service.

The crew consisted of yours truly, president, and Sue, treasurer, a job that entailed no work because money, unfortunately, doesn't grow on trees.

But the aforementioned arboreal appendages do, along with acorns and assorted other nuts, one of whom, as you may have guessed, was me.

I thought I was through with yard work forever when I gave it up several years ago and hired a company to do spring and fall cleanups and, every other week, cut the grass. Or what little there is of it because, thanks to a shady oak in the front, the yard looks like it was manicured with a flamethrower.

Speaking of oaks, they are the root (sorry) of the problem. They are supposedly the strongest trees, but like big, burly, macho guys who faint when they get a flu shot, they're really wimps.

Even in a light breeze, they'll turn into litterbugs, leaving my property strewn with leaves, twigs, branches, acorns, and, in the spring, that disgusting brown gunk that falls on my car, which becomes so messy with sticky stuff that it couldn't be thoroughly cleaned unless I drove it under Niagara Falls.

So you can imagine what my yard looked like after the tropical storm, which should have minded its own business and stayed in the tropics.

The really exasperating part was that countless healthy limbs came crashing down while several dead branches, probably associated with my bank, remained attached to the trunks of our biggest oaks.

I feared that when I went outside to clean up, the trees would know how much this annoyed me and would wait until I was directly underneath, at which point the lifeless limbs would drop on what would soon be my lifeless torso.

After dinner on the day of the storm, Sue and I went out to the front yard and, with one old rake between us, started cleaning up. The rake was of minimal use because it looked like a skinny boxer who'd had a couple of teeth knocked out.

"How come we have only one rake?" I asked Sue.

"Because," she shot back, "you don't do yard work anymore."

So we took turns: One would rake, the other would break up fallen limbs, twigs, and branches and stuff them into a large lawn and garden bag. We worked until dark, then went back in the house, which also was dark.

The next day, I spent five hours cleaning up the backyard, which was a disaster area because it's dotted with oaks that teamed up to see how long it would take me to throw my back out.

I couldn't do that, of course, because it wouldn't have fit in a bag already overflowing with woody debris. Since Sue was out, the only person who could help me was Woody Debris, but he must have been cleaning up his own yard.

A few days later, Sue and I finished the job. All in all, we filled sixteen bags.

As I brought our pathetic little rake back to the shed, a brazen robin taunted me with chirps.

"There's a lesson in all of this," I told Sue. "Tropical storms and mighty oaks are for the birds."

"All Creatures Great and Annoying"

As a longtime practitioner of animal husbandry, which makes me a husband who has had a lot of animals, I love all of God's creatures, except certain creepy insects and other lower life forms, some of whom I have voted for.

Sue, whose husband I am, is even more of an animal lover. She would, I admit, hurt a fly, which is why, flyswatter in hand, she prowls the house in a relentless hunt for the little winged invaders.

But otherwise, she's as gentle as a lamb, one of the few domestic creatures we have not had as pets over the years. Our menagerie has included a dog, a granddog, four cats, several hamsters, half a dozen gerbils, and countless fish, one of which lives in a bowl on the liquor cabinet. I put it there so I could say our fine finny friend drinks like a fish.

But lately Sue has been at war with a pair of squirrels and an indeterminate number of rabbits (the population is uncertain because they breed like rabbits), all of whom are eating her flowers and the fruits and vegetables in her garden.

The squirrels are the worst. Sue thinks they are either siblings or a young married couple honeymooning on our property. I can just see the postcard: "The menu is wonderful. Wish you were here."

I think they are cousins twice removed, though even if I removed them twice, they would return.

The problem is catching them. Because I am afraid of heights and lack a prehensile tail, which fell off when I was in college, I don't climb trees.

Not that it matters because these rambunctious rodents frequently stay on the ground, taunting us. Most normal squirrels would beat a hasty retreat up a nearby oak when they saw a human. Or at least one that looks like me.

Our antagonists sit on the grass and stare directly at us. I could almost hear them say, "Nyah, nyah!" Then again, maybe it's the wind.

The rabbits are just as bad. I've gone out and yelled, "Eh, what's up, doc?" But they just twitch their noses at me. It's infuriating.

Because Sue and I don't want to resort to violence, although I hear there's a sale on dynamite at the Acme Company, we have tried to come up with less harmful means of ridding the yard of these persistent pests.

My sister Elizabeth suggested cutlery.

"We don't want to eat them," I said.

"You don't have to," she replied. "Get some plastic forks and put them in the garden with the tines sticking up. That will discourage the critters."

It worked for a while, until the critters figured out a way to get at Sue's squash and string beans anyway.

"I hate squash, so they can have it," I told Sue. "But I like string beans, so we'll have to try something else."

I suggested putting up a scarecrow with my picture on the face, but Sue said it would be cruelty to animals.

Then there was the coffee ground defense, which entails spreading grounds on the ground. It didn't work.

"No wonder," I said. "The coffee probably kept the critters up all night."

Finally, Sue came up with a solution, which is, ironically, a solution containing water and hot red pepper. It's put into a plastic spray bottle and spritzed on the flowers and whatever grows in the garden, repelling squirrels, rabbits, birds, warthogs, and any other creatures that have designs on your flora.

Unfortunately, it has worked on only one creature.

"Eat your vegetables," Sue said one evening at dinner.

"No, thanks," I replied. "Give them to the squirrels. I'd hate to see any of God's creatures go hungry."

"Beach Blanket Birdbrain"

Whenever I go to the beach, which is about once a year, thus sparing regular beachgoers the horror of witnessing me in a bathing suit, running into the water, and getting eaten by a shark, I imagine myself as Frankie Avalon, star of the "Beach Party" movies of the 1960s.

Sue takes the Annette Funicello role, though she's not very good in it because she doesn't like to dance in the sand — unless, of course, she's bitten by a crab.

So it was with very little fuss, and no rock and roll music, that we staked out a slice of shore, slathered on some sunscreen, and plopped ourselves down in rickety chairs for what was probably the last beach day of the season.

For me, it was the first. And my unexpected presence must have excited a fine feathered flock of aquatic birds because they welcomed me with open wings, which they used to zoom over, past, and around me. One of them squatted nearby, eyeing me with either friendly curiosity or, more likely, open hostility.

It was boy meets gull. We got into a staring contest. I looked over. The bird looked away. I glanced at her out of the corner of my eye (though I don't know how anything round can have a corner) and noticed her staring again.

I made a stupid face. She screeched, which prompted another gull to sit on the opposite side of me. I was surrounded.

I shifted in my chair and almost fell over. The birds flew off and came back moments later with reinforcements, some of which circled overhead before a couple of them dive-bombed me.

I felt like Tippi Hedren in "The Birds."

The only place to escape was the water, but I didn't want to go in because: (a) it looked dirty, (b) it looked cold, and (c) it looked like just the place where Jaws would be waiting for me.

With apologies to John Williams, taking a dip would have been "dumb-dumb, dumb-dumb, dumb-dumb, dumb-dumb."

So, while Sue snoozed and sunbathed, left mercifully alone by my avian adversaries, I got up and walked on the beach. I wore flip-flops to prevent the rocks that studded the shore from hurting my feet, which, even at size eleven, are very delicate.

Speaking of studs, I noticed a couple of young women looking at me. At first I felt like Arnold Schwarzenegger, muscles rippling and glistening in the sun, before I realized that with my physique, I would never be in the male version of the Sports Illustrated swimsuit issue.

Instead, I'd be the cover boy for GQ (Geezers' Quarterly).

I saw a guy with a fishing pole.

"What are you going for?" I asked.

"Porgy and bass," he replied.

"A Gershwin classic," I said, referring to the George Gershwin opera "Porgy and Bess."

For some strange reason, the guy didn't get it. But he did say he also hoped to hook a bull shark, adding: "They're dangerous."

"That's no bull," I stated.

He didn't get that joke, either, so I moseyed back to our little patch of sand, clumps of which became embedded under my nails and between my toes, and plopped down in my chair. I nearly tipped over again, which woke up Sue.

"Let's go," she said.

I struggled to fold the chairs, one of which, I was sure, would slice off a finger. We gathered everything and started to walk back to the parking lot when the birds began harassing me again.

I screeched. One of them whirled to fly away and nearly collided with another one.

I smiled with satisfaction, knowing I probably wouldn't see them again until next year.

As they say at the beach, one bad tern deserves another.

"Going to Seed With a Lawn Guy"

Because I am widely recognized as an airhead, just like the stars of the Tom and Jerry cartoons, you'd think I would be an expert in aeration, which is the process of putting more holes in my yard than I have in my skull.

But it took a lawn service guy (Tom) to show me (Jerry) how to do it right.

"We could have our own show," Tom suggested after he removed the aerator from his truck.

"My granddaughters would be thrilled," I said. "They love Tom and Jerry. Are you going to chase me around with the machine?"

"Not unless you want me to," said Tom, adding: "It would be a cat-and-mouse game."

Chloe and Lilly would have loved that, too, but they probably wouldn't be interested in lawn maintenance, which is why Tom was at my house.

His job was to use the aerator, a hulking, four-hundred-pound, three-thousand-dollar contraption that looks like a giant snow blower, to punch holes in the lawn so water from either the sky or our sprinklers could seep into the ground and, after seeding, allow grass to boldly grow where no grass has grown before.

I watched as Tom revved up the machine, put it in gear, and drove it over the ground in the backyard.

"Could I try?" I asked.

"Sure," said Tom, who is something of a driver's ed instructor for the company's new lawn guys. He showed me how to work the levers — down for drive, up for reverse — and stood back.

I pushed down, the motor roared, and I went flying into a forsythia bush.

"Here, let me help you out of there," said Tom, adding that I didn't have to push the levers all the way down. "Ease them," he instructed as he maneuvered the aerator onto a straight path and let me take the controls again.

This time I didn't floor it and drove like an old man, which I am in real life, except there wasn't a blinker for me to keep on as I tootled along.

"You're doing great," Tom said above the din of the motor as the aerator punched holes in the soft soil.

After I had done a couple of rows, I asked Tom if I could work for the company.

"Why not?" he answered. "We're always hiring."

Tom, who's twenty-five, was hired two years ago.

"Do you take care of your own lawn?" I wondered.

"No," said Tom. "I live with my mom and she doesn't have much of a yard. I take care of other people's yards and they pay me. My mom wouldn't pay me."

"Maybe not," I noted, "but she feeds you."

"That's a pretty good tradeoff," Tom agreed.

Then he showed me how to use a spreader to seed the lawn.

"It's bluegrass and rye," he said of the seeds.

"I thought bluegrass grew only in Kentucky," I said. "And it's a little too early in the day for rye."

Still, the spreader was a lot easier to use than the aerator.

"I've been known to spread fertilizer," I told Tom, who smiled and said, "I think I know what you mean."

Pretty soon, the front and back yards were finished.

"You did a good job," said Tom, adding that it would take two weeks for the seeds to germinate and that I should run the sprinklers for half an hour every day.

"I don't even take a shower every day," I said.

"That's more than I need to know," replied Tom, who said our aerator and spreader adventure could have made a good "Tom and Jerry" episode.

"Let me know when you come back in the spring and I'll make sure my granddaughters are here," I said. "They'll love it."

"They Do an Ice Job"

When it comes to shoveling snow, I am a wuss, which stands for "wait until spring starts."

Unfortunately, I have never been able to convince Sue of this brilliant philosophy in the two-plus decades we have lived in our house.

Sue knows I have been perpetrating snow jobs my whole life. In fact, I was born during a blizzard. So whenever we've had a winter storm, or a nor'easter, or a "snow event," as meteorologists like to say, I have bundled up like I was going on an Arctic expedition and dug out the cars, cleared the front walk, and shoveled the driveway without collapsing into a snowdrift and being found frozen stiff the next morning like Jack Nicholson in "The Shining."

I used to have a small snow blower that turned out to be the Little Engine That Couldn't. My former neighbor Ron would often come over to help me with his large snow blower and kindly gave it to me when he moved, but it, too, has gone to the Great Snowy Beyond.

So I've had to rely on my trusty shovel, which is a glorified soup spoon. I used it to get rid of the eight inches of wet, heavy snow we got during a pre-Christmas storm. After having a shot of blackberry brandy to stave off coronary thrombosis, I finally decided to hire someone to plow the driveway so I could stay inside and get plowed myself.

That brave someone is Justin Felix, nineteen, the wunderkind operator of North Coram Snow Removal.

Justin proved to be a lifesaver (wintergreen, of course) because we recently got fifteen inches of snow that could have stopped a polar bear in its tracks.

Assisting Justin were his father, Nick, forty-eight, a banker who co-founded the side business with Justin several years ago, and Justin's girlfriend, Kate Stevens, eighteen, who worked just as hard and efficiently as the guys.

In fact, Kate wielded a shovel with lightning speed, clearing the front walk in less time than it takes me to put my boots on.

"What's your secret?" I asked.

"I just lift and go," Kate responded.

"If I tried that," I told her, "I'd have to be lifted into an ambulance so I could go to the hospital."

Justin and Nick, meanwhile, each manned a three-stage snow blower that, said Nick, "can cut through ice."

"The ice isn't as thick as my skull, which would probably break the machine," I noted.

Justin smiled and fired up his snow blower, which blew snow (hence, the name) directly into my face when I was stupid enough to stand in the way.

"I have brain freeze," I explained.

Justin, an enterprising young man who also is an investor and works for an affiliate marketing company, started in snow removal when he was fifteen.

"I wanted to help neighbors and make a little bit of money, too," Justin said.

"When I was that age," I told him, "I didn't even help around the house."

That probably makes me the laziest of North Coram's dozen or so customers, some of whom are fellow geezers who have thrown their backs out while trying to throw snow.

"I've also heard some cursing when snowplows leave huge piles at the end of their driveways," Justin said.

I didn't curse, which I have been known to do in such extreme situations, but I did help by moving the cars so the terrific trio could finish clearing my driveway.

"Fantastic job!" I gushed as I paid Justin a very reasonable amount of cold cash. "You just saved me from having a heart attack."

"Next time there's a storm," he promised, "we'll be back."

"Take it from a real flake," I said. "There's no business like your snow business."

"Eggings Over Easy"

I have always been considered a good egg, even though most of my jokes are rotten. That's why I squawked when I found out that chicken-hearted punks had egged a bunch of cars in my neighborhood.

One of those vehicles belongs to Guillaume, who had parked it in my driveway. Feathers ruffled, I called the local police precinct and was connected to a cop whose puns are as criminal as mine.

Officer Vasilecozzo, who works in dispatch, took my complaint over the phone.

"Can you crack the case?" I asked.

"I think so," he replied, presumably with a straight face, "but I wouldn't put all my eggs in one basket."

"These miscreants have obviously run a-fowl of the law," I told him.

"I'll have to scramble to catch them," Officer V said.

"What if they're poachers?" I wondered.

"Then they're on the run," he responded.

"You sound like a hard-boiled detective," I said.

"You're just egging me on," said Officer V.

"Sorry," I said. "I didn't mean to henpeck you."

"Let's end this game of chicken," he said.

"OK," I said. "The beak stops here."

"Good," said Officer V, who began peppering me with questions. "Do you have a Ring camera?" he asked.

"Why," I wanted to know, "are we dealing with a crime ring?"

"If you don't cut this out," he said, "I'm coming over there to wring a confession out of you. Now what else can you tell me?"

Risking incarceration, I said, "There are spent shells in my driveway. And the back of my son-in-law's car is covered in sticky residue. It looks like the work of hardened criminals."

"Or," Officer V said, "they could just be kids on bikes."

I told him that Sue, a fan of TV cop shows, had done some investigating of her own and discovered on her daily walks that only red vehicles had been targeted.

"A red car up the street was egged," I said. "And a red truck around the corner was also hit."

"What color is your son-in-law's car?" Officer V asked.

"Red," I said.

"He must be seeing red," the cop quipped.

"He's blue in the face," I remarked.

Officer V said he would file a report and asked me to get back to him if anything else happened.

That night, Guillaume's car was egged again. The next day, I called the precinct and spoke with Officer V.

"You must be shellshocked," he said.

"I'm walking on eggshells," I told him. "I'd like to see these guys fry."

"That would never pan out," he assured me.

"The eggs stink," I said. "If this were a cop show, it would be 'Law & Odor.' "

Officer V said his favorite cop show is "Lucifer."

"I haven't seen that one," I said.

"It's really good," he told me. "But so far, none of the episodes have been about egg throwers."

"What are you going to do about the ones in my neighborhood?" I asked.

"We'll send out a patrol car," Officer V promised. "Maybe the police presence will be enough to deter them from continuing their messy activities."

"Will you let me know if you make any arrests?" I said.

"Don't worry," he said. "If we catch these guys, the yolk will be on them."

Officer V's plan seems to have worked because there haven't been any further eggings.

When I called back to thank him, Officer V declined to take credit and said a coordinated effort between police and the community is what helps stem such quality-of-life crimes.

"Don't be so modest," I told him. "This is really a feather in your cap."

"I appreciate it," said Officer V. "But more than likely, these guys just chickened out."

"Pole Dancing With the Stars"

I may be happily married to the most beautiful woman on Earth (she'd be number one on other planets, too), but it has always been on my bucket list to meet a pole dancer.

My wish came true when I made the acquaintance of Brandyn Phillips, a fully dressed guy who got into a bucket so he could install a new utility pole in my backyard.

"Your idea of a pole dancer has a whole different meaning," said Brandyn, who was assisted by Robert Frederick Higgins III, known on the crew as Rob 1, and Robert Baldeo, aka Rob 2.

The terrific trio came over to replace an old pole on which was attached lines that provide power to homes throughout the neighborhood. The mission was to remove the lines and put them on the new pole, which had to be sunk in the corner of the yard before the old pole was removed.

"Can you dance?" I asked Brandyn.

"Yes," he replied. "But I'd never do it in the bucket. And I'd keep my clothes on."

"Nobody would want to see you without them," said Rob 1. "The neighbors would call the cops."

"He'd have to use the tips for bail money," Rob 2 chimed in.

Rob 1 ranks ahead of Rob 2 because he has been on the job longer.

"You're just a heartbeat away from being Rob 1," I told Rob 2.

"I don't like the sound of that!" said Rob 1.

Neither one had to risk his life by going up in the bucket — that's Brandyn's job. He became a friend in high places when he told me that his tallest order was being three hundred and fifty feet in the air while working on wind turbines in Iowa, his home state.

"The highest I've ever worked on power lines is one hundred and eighty feet," said Brandyn, adding that the lines on the pole in my yard are a mere twenty-nine feet up.

"I'm afraid of being any higher off the ground than the top of my head," I told him.

Perhaps because my noggin is filled with air, I asked if I could go up in the bucket. Brandyn politely said no because of safety rules.

"If I fell out and landed on my head," I said, "I wouldn't get hurt."

"I don't doubt that," said Brandyn, who did let me climb into the bucket, which was plastered with "Danger" signs. I found out why when I slipped while trying to lift one leg over the edge and almost qualified to be the lead singer for the Vienna Boys' Choir.

When I finally got in, I saw all the tools that Brandyn uses to switch lines, which he did after the bucket — without me in it — was lifted to the top of the old pole by a huge vehicle with tank wheels and a boom that was operated from the ground by Rob 1.

"Can I drive it?" I asked.

"You wouldn't get very far," Rob 1 replied.

"I'm fat," said Rob 2, who weighs three hundred pounds, "and I can walk faster."

But first, the thirty-five-foot-tall new pole had to be driven six feet into the ground.

"If it fell on me," I said, "I'd be six feet under."

After Brandyn switched the lines, which carry seven thousand six hundred and twenty volts, the old pole had to be removed.

"If you want to be useful," Rob 1 said, "grab a shovel and start digging."

"I work dirt cheap," I said.

At that moment, Sue came outside and said, "What are you doing?"

"I'm helping out," I responded.

"You're bothering these guys," she said.

"And he's doing a damn good job," Rob 2 assured her.

At least I didn't get electrocuted, which would have prompted my final words: "That's all, volts!"

But I did assist three great guys in keeping the power on in my neighborhood.

As I told Sue after they left, "Now I can take pole dancing off my bucket list."

CHAPTER 3

(The expression "shop till you drop" doesn't apply to me. I'd rather drop before I shop so I don't have to go. But as every retiree knows, sometimes there's just no escape from a trip to the store.)

"This Customer Is Always Right"

As a "valued customer," which is better than being a "customer nobody cares about," I can't go to the store to buy a toothbrush without being asked to fill out a survey.

The survey is usually at the end of a receipt that is long enough to encircle my car, in which I drive home so I can go online and answer questions about the store, the service, and, of course, my new toothbrush.

Sometimes I receive an email from the store, asking: "How did we do?"

Then I am expected to take the survey again.

Stores aren't the only places that want to know how I feel about them. I also am asked to fill out surveys from the bank, the post office, the pharmacy, the supermarket, and other places that want my opinion, which in my own home is regarded as worthless.

One of these days, I'll get a survey from the lunatic asylum, which is where I will end up if I keep getting requests to fill out surveys.

It made me wonder: If all these places want to know what I think of them, what do they think of me as a "valued customer"?

So I conducted my own surveys.

I started at the post office, where Kenny asked how he could help me. I told him I wanted to mail an envelope containing a book.

"Are the contents potentially hazardous?" he asked.

"It's a book I wrote," I replied, "so the contents are potentially hazardous if you read it."

Kenny smiled, gave me a "media rate," and handed me a receipt with a tracking number and — you guessed it — a survey.

"You're an exemplary employee," I told Kenny. "But how am I as a customer?"

"I really can't complain," he answered. "So far, so good. You did well. I'll give you a good review."

I thanked Kenny and went to the bank, where I was helped by Ranisha.

"I have two checks totaling $44.47," I said. "I'd like to deposit them. I'm sorry they aren't for a million dollars, but every little bit helps."

Ranisha chuckled and said, "With interest, you might become a millionaire after all."

When the transaction was completed, I said I was taking a survey.

"Am I a good customer?" I asked.

"You're very good and very nice," she said. "I give you high marks."

Later, I asked Maria, my barber, to rate me as a customer.

"You're great," she said as she snipped my wiry locks. "You're polite, punctual, and considerate. What more could I ask for? You're doing very well. In fact, you're a dream."

"Some dreams are nightmares," I noted.

"You're not one of them," said Maria, whom I have known for twenty years.

"How would I rank on a survey?" I inquired.

"You'd get top marks," Maria said.

For my last survey, I headed to the store to buy a toothbrush and spoke with Christina, whom I also have known for twenty years.

"When you started coming in, I was in the photo department. Now I'm a shift supervisor," Christina said. "I owe it all to you."

When I asked her to rate me as a customer, Christina said, "You're the hostess with the mostest! I'd absolutely give you high marks."

I got a toothbrush and brought it to the counter.

"Are you ready to check out?" Christina asked.

"Not for many more years," I responded.

"You are too much!" said Christina, who handed me a long receipt. "You can wear it as a scarf," she suggested.

"Thanks for taking my survey," I said.

"I wish we had surveys to rank customers," said Christina. "A lot of them would get bad marks."

"How about me?" I asked.

"Believe me," Christina said, "nobody could top you."

"Sole Searching at the Shoe Store"

As a man who likes to put one foot in front of the other, which works pretty well until I walk headlong into a wall, I have always valued comfort over style when it comes to what I wear on my tremendously ticklish tootsies.

That's why it was a big (size eleven) deal when I went shopping for slippers.

Slippers are the preferred footwear for retirees like myself who don't have to don dress shoes for work or sneakers for playing sports at which I was always terrible and that would induce cardiac arrest if I played them now. These items cost an arm and a leg, which isn't too practical since I'd need the former to pay for them and the latter to wear them.

But slippers are cheap and cozy for lying around the house or padding to the refrigerator for beer. They can even be worn to throw out the garbage or pick up take-out pizza.

"You need a new pair," said Sue, pointing out that my slippers not only had gaping holes in the toes but smelled bad enough to asphyxiate a camel.

So we drove to a store that specializes in biped impedimenta.

"I'm looking for slippers," I told a sales associate named Doris.

"They're right next to you," she said pleasantly, indicating a shelf full of them.

I pulled out a box of slippers in my size and asked if I could try them on.

"Of course," Doris said.

"On my bare feet?" I wondered.

"We have little stockings you can wear," said Doris.

"Maybe they'll bring out my feminine side," I said.

"We also have high heels," Doris informed me.

"They'd be dangerous after a couple of beers," I noted.

I sat on a bench, took off my socks, and yanked on the little stockings, but I couldn't cram my right foot into the corresponding slipper.

"The size must be wrong," I grumbled.

Sue sighed and said, "Take the paper ball out of the front."

"Sorry," I said sheepishly. "I don't go shopping too often."

"Now you know why I go by myself," said Sue, who noticed that the slippers, which fit fine, were different colors.

"One's light and one's dark," Doris agreed. "Try another pair and see if they match."

I grabbed a box containing only one slipper.

"It's for my left foot," I said. "I have two left feet, which is why I'm not on 'Dancing With the Stars.' "

Doris handed me another box, which contained two slippers, and said, "Try these."

I slipped them on and said, "They fit like gloves."

"Please," Sue begged, anticipating my next comment, "don't say anything else."

Instead, I extolled the virtue of slippers for the geezer set and said I sometimes run errands in them.

"Why not?" Doris said. "Nobody looks at your feet anyway."

"Even my wife doesn't like to look at my feet," I said.

Sue politely did not disagree.

When I told Doris I'm retired, she said, "I retired from my job in social services eight years ago. This," she added, referring to her part-time gig at the store, "is my casino money."

Doris said she's sixty-nine and has "three children, five grandchildren, and, I think, four great-grandchildren."

"Is your husband retired?" I asked.

"No, I got myself a young dude," said Doris, who is twenty years older.

"When he gets to be my age," I said, noting that I'm sixty-six, "he'll come to appreciate slippers."

I chose the last pair I tried on and thanked Doris for her help.

"Now I can throw out my smelly old ones," I told her. "And when I get take-out pizza, I'll go in style."

"Supermarket Driving Test"

If you are a senior (and I'm not talking about a high school kid who got a car as a graduation gift), your driving skills have probably diminished so much that you can barely operate the simplest of vehicles.

By that I mean shopping carts.

Since I am the designated cart driver when I go grocery shopping with Sue, I have devised a test to help you safely navigate your local supermarket.

I came up with the idea when Sue and I went shopping and encountered so many rude, reckless, and maddeningly clueless cart operators that they all should have been pulled over, given a hefty ticket, and had their driver's licenses suspended.

Good luck!

QUESTION 1

If you are in the produce aisle and are cut off by another cart driver who then goes at a snail's pace, what should you do?

(a) Hit him with a cantaloupe.
(b) Pull out your cellphone and call 911.
(c) Leave your cart in the middle of the aisle and go home.

ANSWER: None of the above. Just stand there and fume. Or, better yet, forget the fruits and veggies and go to the next aisle. Who needs broccoli anyway?

QUESTION 2

Speaking of cellphones, should you text and drive in the supermarket?

ANSWER: Not unless your spouse isn't with you and you need to call home every three minutes to ask where everything on your shopping list is.

QUESTION 3

Who drives worse, men or women?

ANSWER: Both can be pretty bad, but at least women know where they are going. That is why they are more likely to speed, weave in and out of traffic, and create chaos in the frozen food section, where they often stop to get ice cream.

Men, for the most part, have absolutely no idea where they are going, what they are doing, or why they are even in the supermarket, although most of them know instinctively where the beer is.

QUESTION 4

If you are the designated cart driver and you can't keep up with your spouse on the way to the deli counter, or you have just been involved in a fender bender with a little old lady who is looking for prune juice, what should you do?

(a) Stand in the aisle and block traffic.
(b) Pull over to the side and block other shoppers from getting items you are standing in front of.
(c) Go immediately to the beer section.

ANSWER: (c)

QUESTION 5

What safety features are standard equipment in shopping carts?

ANSWER: None. Carts don't have power steering, which makes them difficult to operate since they all have four wheels that go in different directions. Also, they don't have backup cameras, which makes it difficult to see the cart that is parked right behind you.

QUESTION 6

Why aren't there traffic cops in supermarkets?

ANSWER: Good question.

QUESTION 7

Why aren't cart drivers required to have insurance?

ANSWER: Another good question.

QUESTION 8

Is parallel parking even possible in a supermarket?

ANSWER: No.

QUESTION 9

What should you do if you are involved in an aisle rage incident?

ANSWER: See answer to Question 4.

QUESTION 10

When you are at the checkout counter, what should you do?

(a) Get in the express lane with more than the allotted twelve items.
(b) Realize you don't have your debit card and struggle to find a pen so you can write a check.
(c) Take half an hour to bag your groceries.
(d) All of the above.

ANSWER: (d)

BONUS QUESTION

What should you do the next time you have to go to the supermarket?

ANSWER: Stay home and drink the beer you bought the last time you went shopping.

"The Bucks Stop Here"

A major American bank where I don't have any money because, unfortunately, I don't have any money has hired Jennifer Garner and Samuel L. Jackson, major American actors who have a lot more money than I do, to ask me this important financial question:

"What's in your wallet?"

The answer, Jennifer and Samuel L., is three dollars.

But at least it is tucked into a brand-new wallet I just bought because my old wallet was falling apart despite the lamentable fact that there was never much money in it.

Sue, who manages the money in our house, where we still live because she pays the mortgage every month, took me shopping at a store that specializes in handbags, luggage, and accessories such as wallets that really ought to hold more than three dollars.

"Is there any money in here?" I asked the very nice, witty, and helpful store manager, Laurabeth Collins, as I peeked inside one of the wallets on display.

"No, I took it out," Laurabeth replied. "You should have come this morning."

"I may buy it anyway because I need a new one," I said, taking out my old wallet to show Laurabeth.

"I've seen worse," she told me.

"The problem," I said, "is that it's too thick, like my skull, but it hurts the opposite end when I sit down."

Laurabeth nodded and said, "If you don't have any money in there, what's making it so thick?"

"Cards," I answered. "Credit cards, insurance cards, Medicare cards, appointment cards, everything except playing cards, which would make the wallet even thicker except I'm not playing with a full deck."

Laurabeth nodded again and said, "I can save you some money and solve your card problem at the same time."

"How?" I asked eagerly.

"With a wallet set, which costs less than just this one wallet," she said, showing me a box with a wallet, a card insert, and a keychain. "You can carry the card insert separately," Laurabeth noted, "so your opposite end won't hurt when you sit down."

"That would be good for the bottom line," I said.

Sue and Laurabeth exchanged glances.

"Or," said Laurabeth, "maybe you'd like a sling bag."

"What's it for," I asked, "a slingshot?"

"No," Laurabeth said. "It's for guys who have too much stuff. My husband is always saying to me, 'Put this in your bag, put that in your bag.' I told him, 'Get your own!' "

"You mean it's like a pocketbook for men?" I asked.

"It's more like a small backpack," Laurabeth said as she showed me some. "Then there are man bags, which are bigger."

"What do women carry credit cards in?" I inquired.

"Zip-around wallets," Sue answered. "I love mine."

"Me, too!" Laurabeth said in a wifely bonding. "I also keep my membership cards in there."

"I don't belong anywhere," I admitted.

"Poor guy," Laurabeth said sympathetically.

"No, I mean I belong at home," I said, looking at Sue for assurance, "but I don't belong to a health club or any other place that would have to lower its standards to accept me."

"That means your card insert won't be too thick," said Sue, who suggested I get the wallet set. "And if you don't use the keychain, I'll take it."

"Sold!" I told Laurabeth, who also sold me a shaving kit at a big discount.

"This is your lucky day," she said. "You got a wallet set and a shaving kit and you saved a lot of money."

"And I still have three dollars left over," I said.

"What are you going to spend it on?" Laurabeth asked.

"Lottery tickets," I answered. "I want to have a good answer the next time Jennifer Garner and Samuel L. Jackson ask me what's in my wallet."

"Under the Influence"

I have very little influence, even in my own home, which is the only place where I am a household name, but that won't stop me from achieving my new and extremely dubious goal of being one of the most influential people in the world.

That's right: I want to be an influencer.

Until recently, I didn't know that influencers existed. Then I started reading about alleged celebrities who possess no discernible talent but are rich and, even more important, famous for being famous, despite the curious fact that they are not famous enough for me to have ever heard of them.

Still, they are making boatloads of money, which they presumably use to buy boats, by endorsing products that their zillions of social media followers will buy, thus giving them (the influencers) even more money.

I may not be rich, or have zillions of social media followers, or possess any discernible talent beyond the frightening ability to make stupid jokes at the drop of a hat, which I will pick up for you and put on my own head, but I do have one thing most influencers sorely lack: an excellent reputation.

I found this out when I saw that MyLife, an American information brokerage firm that gathers personal info on people through public records and other sources, has given me a score of 4.22 out of five, which is six percent above the national average.

When I told Sue about this impressive news, she said, "Do they have the right person?"

It was a good question because in order to get a full report, I will have to pay a fee that could be more than I will make as an influencer. Nonetheless, I know that my reputation is higher than that of most people, which makes you wonder who the hell they are and whether they are incarcerated.

Because I am a free man, and worth every penny, I have looked into products I could influence shamefully gullible people to purchase.

In my extensive research, which has so far covered approximately a minute and a half, I have discovered that influencers like to hawk jewelry. Aside from my wedding ring, which I got in 1978, I don't wear jewelry.

Influencers, most of whom are decades younger than I am, also peddle skin-care products such as moisturizers. As a bona fide geezer, I don't think even a tub of Turtle Wax would help remove my wrinkles.

So I came up with a product that not only is a boon to mankind, but one I use all the time: beer.

I once made my own beer, Jerry's Nasty Ale, which went down smooth and came back up the same way. I don't dare make another batch, so I decided to contact a company that produces a beer that has both excellent quality and a national reputation.

That's why I called Samuel Adams (the brewery, not the dead patriot, who doesn't answer his phone) to ask if I could be an influencer.

"We don't have a formal influencer program," said Brittany Zahoruiko, who oversees public relations for the company. "We'd have to take it on a case-by-case basis."

"Did you say 'case-by-case'?" I asked delightedly.

"I think I did," Brittany replied, suddenly realizing she had made a beer pun. "I didn't even mean to."

In my case, being a Sam Adams influencer probably won't work out.

But I know someone else who would be a good influencer for any product because her reputation is even better than mine: Sue.

On MyLife, she scored 4.76 out of five, which is twelve percent above the national average.

"That's twice as good as yours," Sue said before asking me to take out the garbage.

"Yes, dear," I replied. "In our house, at least, you have a lot of influence."

"Smooth Selling in the Showroom"

Because I am a man who couldn't sell snow shovels in Alaska, surfboards in Hawaii, or beer in Death Valley (I'd drink it first), I never thought I could sell cars to anybody but myself. And because my driveway is short and my garage is full of junk, where would I put them all?

So I decided to visit the best salesman I know, James Boyd, of Hyundai 112 in Medford, New York, to see how it's done.

James, who's forty-two and has been in the business for twenty years, has sold me my last two cars, both SUVs named for Santa Fe, another place where I couldn't sell anything, even the artwork for which the city is famous.

"Welcome, JZEE!" James exclaimed when I entered the showroom on a busy weekday afternoon. He calls me by that name (pronounced Jay-Z, like the rapper, except I'm the original) because that's what is on my license plates, which Sue got for me several years ago. "They're the best I've ever seen," James said. "Now, what can I do for you? Do you want another car?"

"Not yet," I said. "But since I'm retired, and have nothing better to do, and need to get out of Sue's hair, I thought I'd try to sell cars."

"You've come to the right place," said James, who then excused himself to take care of some of the many customers he had that day.

While he was gone, I struck up a conversation with two of them, Vickie and Bret, who were there to pick up a car James had sold to them a couple of days before.

"James is very good," Bret said. "He's friendly, knowledgeable, and professional."

"We planned to go to another dealership after this," Vickie added, "but we met James and we never left this one."

Just then, James came back to his desk to pick up some paperwork.

"You're supposed to be making the plates," he told me.

"I'll probably end up doing it in prison," I said. "And I should have a plate in my head. By the way, do I get a commission for talking with these nice people?"

"We'll see about that," James said before dashing off again.

"You'll owe him money," Bret said.

"Could I be a salesman?" I asked.

"Sure," Vickie said. "You chat up customers, you have a good personality and a great sense of humor, and you're outgoing. You could sell anything."

Vickie should know because she works in sales at a home improvement store.

I decided to try out my sales technique on Bret when Vickie said he would be getting their old car and she'd get the new one.

"Why should you drive the old one when you can have a beautiful, brand-new car just like Vickie got?" I told him.

"No!" he said firmly.

"Think of the prestige," I said.

"Think of the money," Bret replied.

When James returned again, I asked, "Who's your best customer?"

"You, JZEE!" he said.

"And now I want to be your best salesman," I said, though I knew I could never be as good as James because, as he has told me, he loves his job and enjoys working with people, and that the secret of his success is having a good sense of humor, not putting pressure on customers, being straightforward, and working hard to make them happy.

"Did you sell Bret a car?" James asked.

"I'm trying," I said.

"I'll tell you what," James said as he handed Vickie the keys to her new car and the delightful couple started to leave. "If Bret buys one, you can have the commission."

"What do you say, Bret?" I said.

"I'll think about it," he replied.

"They're going fast," I said.

"OK," Bret said. "I'll come back."

"And when you do," I said, "just ask for JZEE."

"Put a Cork In It"

I am a connoisseur of fine wines, and have the liquor store bills to prove it, so I can say with great authority and a slight hangover that when it comes to pairing wine and food, reds go with Slim Jims and whites go with Twinkies.

For this impressive expertise, I am known to oenophiles, Francophiles, and especially juveniles as a real corker. But until recently, I had never corked wine or even bottled the stuff.

So I went to Shinn Estate Vineyards in Mattituck, New York, to see how the professionals do it.

My instructor was Patrick Caserta, Shinn's talented winemaker, who was working with Jon Sidewitz, Carlos Magana, and Rosa Ulan to bottle and cork two hundred and thirty cases of cabernet franc.

"Would you like some?" Patrick asked.

"It's ten o'clock in the morning," I pointed out.

"Wine for breakfast is pretty good," Patrick said.

"Cheers!" I replied as I sipped and savored the fruity red nectar.

"This cab franc has been aged in a stainless steel tank for a short time," Patrick explained. "It's young."

"Unlike me," I said. "I've been fermenting for almost seven decades."

"You have quite a vintage," Patrick noted.

"It's just sour grapes," I said.

The grapes in Patrick's cabernet were anything but sour. In fact, they were wonderfully refreshing.

"When we harvest these grapes, we don't add sulfur," Patrick told me. "It's a fruitier kind of wine that should be chilled at cellar temperature."

"I don't have a cellar," I said.

"Then you should drink it right away," Patrick said.

I stuck my large nose in the small glass that contained the cab franc, inhaled without drowning, and swallowed the rest of the wine.

"It tickles the palate," I declared.

"It also tickles the pallets," said Patrick, adding that each one holds sixty cases.

"I rest my case," I told him.

"Good," said Patrick. "Now you can help bottle and cork the wine."

The bottling part involved putting an empty glass container under an apparatus that would feed the wine into the bottle.

"You have to fit the top of the bottle against the rubber seal," Patrick instructed. "If you don't do it right, the bottle will keep filling and the wine will spray all over like a geyser."

"With me," I said, "it would be a geyser on a geezer."

No such mishap occurred because I put the bottle directly into the seal and watched as the wine flowed freely and flawlessly, stopping exactly at the top.

"Nice job!" exclaimed Patrick, who said the wine was being pumped from a tank by gravity.

"Sir Isaac Newton must have discovered it when a grape fell on his head," I theorized.

Patrick nodded and began to tell me about ethyl acetate.

"Who's she?" I wondered.

"The wife of Norman Acetate," replied Patrick, adding that it's an organic compound in fermentation.

After my successful bottling, I attempted to put a cork in it. This entailed bringing the bottle to the corking machine, pressing a thin metal trigger, and watching the cork be plunged snugly into the top of the bottle.

"You're a real pro!" said Patrick, who's forty-six.

"You were born when I reached the legal drinking age," I said.

"No wonder you're so good at this," said Patrick, who let me fill and cork several more bottles. "You've put your blood, sweat, and tears into it."

"Maybe this batch should be known as Cabernet Jerry," I suggested.

"You can tell Mrs. Zezima you had a hand in it," Patrick said, referring to Sue, who, like me, is a Shinn Wine Club member.

"What about Franc?" I asked.

"We won't tell him," said Patrick, adding that my cab would pair well with chicken or hamburgers.

"It's the best wine I've ever had," I gushed. "I can't wait to try it with Slim Jims."

"This Guy's a Real Card"

If I ever got a job at Hallmark, the greeting card company that helps people express their true feelings on such important occasions as birthdays, anniversaries, and holidays like National Beer Day, which is April 7 but for me can be any day, I'd suggest a line of humorous sympathy cards. Like this one:

> *Violets are blue,*
> *Roses are red.*
> *Sorry to hear*
> *Your goldfish is dead.*

Now you know why Hallmark would never lower its otherwise high standards to pay me actual money to write greeting cards. But there should be some interest in hiring Sue, who has started writing her own greetings, which she calls Nini's Homemade Cards.

She made the first one for me on Valentine's Day. Instead of buying a card, which would keep Hallmark in business, Sue folded a sheet of pink construction paper in half, cut out a red and pink heart from other sheets of paper, glued it to the front of the card, and wrote this sentiment inside:

> *Roses are red,*
> *Violets are blue.*
> *I made this valentine*
> *Just for you!!*
> *Happy Valentine's Day!*
> *Love you!!*
> *Sue*

Not quite as moving as my dead-goldfish card, but I appreciated her effort. So, more recently, did Xavier and Chloe, for whom Sue, known to all five of our grandkids as Nini, made colorful birthday cards, even using sparkles on the covers.

Such brilliant creativity made me think Sue could work for Hallmark. So I called the company and was put in touch with Andrew Blackburn, who writes greeting cards for a living.

"What your wife has done with her cards is impossible at Hallmark," said Blackburn, thirty-two, who has been writing for the company for eleven years.

"Wow, I guess that means she's unique," I said.

"What makes what your wife did meaningful and special is that she took the time to do it herself," Blackburn said diplomatically. "But what we have to do is not only tap into what makes a card meaningful to an individual person, but tap into universal specifics."

"It sounds like she wouldn't be an ideal fit at Hallmark," I said.

"They're smart enough not to let me make those decisions," said Blackburn, a personable guy who has created some outstanding cards, including a Father's Day classic.

On the cover, which features a picture of a smiling brother and sister on a swing, it says: "A good dad lets his kids play outside."

On the inside, it says: "A great dad lets them back in. Happy Father's Day to a great dad."

"I don't remember if I wrote that one before I had kids or after," said Blackburn, who has two sons, ages six and four. "But now there are moments when I realize the truth of it."

He also realizes he is in a unique position never to forget his wedding anniversary.

"I write greeting cards, so I'd have no excuse," said Blackburn, who has been happily married to his wife, Becca, for as long as he has been working at Hallmark.

"She's super supportive and loves what I do," he said.

"Would she be interested in writing greeting cards like my wife does?" I wondered.

"No," said Blackburn. "She leaves that to me."

"I think Sue will leave that you, too," I said. "That way, she can continue to write cards for the family and you can keep your job."

"It's a win-win," Blackburn said.

"Maybe you can start writing cards for such important holidays as National Beer Day," I suggested. "And don't forget those humorous sympathy cards."

"Don't worry," Blackburn said. "If your goldfish dies, you will have my sympathy."

CHAPTER 4

(Grandchildren make retirement grand — except when you can't see them in person to hug, kiss, or play with. The pandemic kept Sue and me away from our quintet of cuties for months. FaceTime is good, but it's no substitute for the real thing.)

"A Grandfather's Guide to Physical Fitness"

As an out-of-shape geezer who drinks red wine to avoid heart trouble and believes that exercise and health food will kill you, I am proud, happy, and practically comatose to report that I got the best workout I've had in months. And with not one but two personal trainers.

I refer, naturally, to my granddaughters.

Because of coronavirus restrictions, I hadn't seen Chloe, seven, and Lilly, four, since the summer. And we had to wear masks and keep a safe social distance.

Sue and I had to do the same this time, when we watched the girls for a couple of hours while Lauren, a talented photographer who has her own business, Lauren Demolaize Photography, was out on a photo shoot.

The fun, frolic, and potential cardiac issues included:

Running around the backyard in a spirited and nearly debilitating game of tag.

Playing catch with a rubber ball.

Playing catch with a plastic ball.

Kicking a soccer ball.

Chasing and popping bubbles as they floated through the air.

Writhing spasmodically in a failed effort to keep a hula hoop going for more than three seconds at a time.

Pushing Lilly on a swing, running around to stand in front of her, and dashing back to push her again when she said she wasn't going high enough.

Falling to the ground and pretending to be knocked unconscious by Chloe's high-kick swinging.

Sprinting next to the girls as they zoomed down the slide, which they did, one after the other, about a dozen times.

Throwing each girl into the air and catching her while trying not to rupture a vital organ.

And, what we boomers call the sport of kinks, playing horsey, a game in which yours truly was the horse (instead of my usual role as the back end of one). I got down on my hands and knees while both girls jumped on my back and exhorted me to giddyup, which I did, slowly and pathetically, uphill and downhill, until I collapsed in a heap, after which the girls wanted me to give them another ride. As my entire skeletal structure started to crumble, I wondered: They shoot horses, don't they?

Needless to say, but I'll say it anyway, we had a blast. Unbounded exuberance and the narrow avoidance of hospitalization are what happens when grandparents and their grandchildren finally get together after weeks of being separated.

Since we all wore masks and were outside, Sue and I were able to get closer to the girls than we would if we were in the house, but we still had to be careful. The granddaughter tosses and the horsey rides were done while we faced away from each other.

Nonetheless, Chloe and Lilly could run an open-air health club. And I, a hip grandfather hoping not to be a broken-hip grandfather, or even a hip-replacement grandfather, could be their first, best, and most ancient customer.

"You're fun, Poppie!" Chloe said as I gasped for air after one of our strenuous exercises.

"Even though you're old!" Lilly added helpfully.

After Lauren returned, Sue and I drove home, where we wolfed down dinner and watched a movie, during which I nodded off so often that I must have looked like a bobblehead doll.

"You got quite a workout today," Sue said as she turned off the TV and we headed up to bed.

"At least you didn't have to call 911," I noted.

"It was like being at the gym," Sue said.

"I hope it's not another several months before I can join," I replied. "And when I do, the girls can push me on a swing and give me a senior citizen discount."

"To Have and Have Knocks"

Knock, knock.

Who's there?

Jerry.

Jerry who?

Jerry Christmas and happy New Year!

OK, so I just made up this lame attempt at humor, but that doesn't mean it shouldn't be included in the next edition of "Knock, Knock! The Biggest, Best Joke Book Ever," which Sue and I gave to Chloe for holiday ho, ho, hos.

Since then, Chloe, who's seven and a half and loves to laugh, which not only is true but also rhymes, has been calling me with knock, knock jokes.

"Knock, knock," Chloe said in her most recent call.

"Who's there?" I answered.

"Weirdo," said Chloe.

"Weirdo who?" I replied, convinced she was talking about me.

"Weirdo you think you're going?"

"Ha ha!" we laughed in unison.

Chloe and her little sister, Lilly, who's four and is a real pistol, with a sassy sense of humor and a mischievous grin, not only love to tell me jokes but routinely invite me to parties on FaceTime, which is the closest we get to seeing each other — without face masks and social distancing — in this age of viral quarantine.

"Poppie?" Lilly said on the screen while dressed like a fairy princess.

"Yes, honey?" I replied while attired in my pajamas.

"What's Pinocchio's name when he tells a joke?"

"What?"

"Pin-JOKE-io!"

All three of us laughed at the witticism, which Lilly obviously made up all by herself. I was so proud of her!

People often ask me if I spoil my grandchildren.

"No," I tell them. "That's my wife's job. My job is to corrupt them."

I must admit, with all due modesty, that I have succeeded splendidly. That was evident at our latest virtual party.

"Knock, knock," Chloe said.

"Who's there?" I replied.

"Owl."

"Owl who?"

"Owl be seeing you!"

More giggling.

"We're having a picnic," Lilly announced.

"What can I bring?" I asked.

"You can bring the telephone," Lilly instructed.

Chloe, who like me was still in her pajamas, except hers were adorned with a castle while mine sported coffee stains, was eating a small bag of pita chips. So was Lilly. I had a bag of Bambas.

"Here, Lilly," I said, pretending to feed her one of the peanut snacks through the screen.

"It's in my head!" Lilly squealed.

Chloe and I chortled.

Lilly was on a roll, which didn't surprise me because I had heard from Lauren that when she scolded Lilly for making a mess in the house, Lilly retorted: "You're fired!"

"Lilly," I said. "Did you fire Mommy?"

"Yes," she responded, very seriously, without explanation.

I burst out laughing. Chloe laughed, too. Lilly kept a straight face for a few seconds. Then came that mischievous grin. She looked into the camera and said, "Poppie?"

"Yes, Lilly?"

53

"You're a knucklehead!"

We all roared. At least I wasn't fired.

While all this frivolity was going on, I was sipping coffee out of the mug the girls gave me for Christmas. It says: "Dad Jokes: Served fresh daily."

But the jokes were on me.

"Knock, knock," Chloe said.

"Who's there?"

"Boo."

"Boo who?"

"Don't cry, it's just a joke."

I laughed.

"Knock, knock," Chloe said again.

"Who's there?"

"Olive."

"Olive who?"

Chloe smiled and said, "Olive you."

I smiled back and said, "Olive you, too."

Olive both girls, who have inherited Poppie's propensity for jokes, silliness, and just plain fun.

Someday, when this pandemic is over, we'll get together and have a real party. Then we'll open the book and tell each other jokes.

Take it from a goofy grandfather who graduated, magna cum laughter, from the School of Funny Knocks.

"The Poppie Show"

If there's one good thing that can be said about the pandemic (the bad things can't be repeated here), it's that it has kept me off the streets.

That means, unfortunately, that I can't get out to see my grandchildren. So I have stayed home and become a TV star.

"The Poppie Show," named for me because all five kids call me Poppie (adults call me things that also can't be repeated here), airs regularly on FaceTime. It's an interactive, on-demand program that allows me and the children to see each other, something we haven't done in person, in the case of the youngest three, for more than a year.

What's worse is that the youngest two are twins who are a year and a half old, so it will give you some idea of what I have been missing.

The same goes for Sue, whom the kids call Nini. She's sometimes a guest on "The Poppie Show." It helps boost the ratings.

One recent episode began when I got a call from Katie, who said that Zoe, one of the twins, was saying "Poppie" and wanted to see me.

Zoe popped up on the phone screen with a big smile.

"Hi, Zoe!" I gushed, smiling back at her. "It's Poppie!"

Katie held up a family photo collage and asked Zoe, "Where's Poppie?"

Zoe pointed to my picture and said, "Poppie!"

Her younger (by twenty-five minutes) brother, Quinn, also popped up on the screen, flashing a big smile. He said my name, too.

"They've joined the Cult of Poppie," said Katie, whose son Xavier has been a member for all of his nearly four years.

Xavier sent me an original artwork for my birthday. Before that, he sent me another watercolor he made all by himself. It's modern art, so I don't know exactly what is depicted, but both pieces are beautiful. Since I don't have enough postage to donate them to the Louvre, I taped them to the wall in my office at home.

Naturally, the drawings were featured on "The Poppie Show."

"He wanted to send them to you," said Katie, who, in an earlier episode, told me to watch the mail.

"For you, Poppie," Xavier said.

It was the highlight of the show, which is billed as a comedy (the laughs are at my expense since I'm less mature than the children), but there is some drama, too, because Sue and I see how much the kids, especially Zoe and Quinn, have grown but sadly can't be there to toddle along with them.

The last time we saw them in person, right after New Year's of 2020, Xavier was toddling and the twins were infants.

Chloe, who's almost eight, and her sister, Lilly, four, are frequent guests on "The Poppie Show." In fact, they call me all the time so we can sing, dance, and be silly, which adds considerably to the entertainment value of the program.

Lauren sometimes makes a cameo appearance, usually in the background while she cooks dinner or cleans the house.

Sue and I have visited the girls a couple of times in recent months, since they live a lot closer to us than Xavier, Zoe, and Quinn, whom we have to get on an airplane to visit. We stay outside, we keep a safe social distance, and we all wear masks. But most of the time, we see each other on the small screen.

One of these days, everyone will be vaccinated, the pandemic will be over, and I can see, hug, kiss, sing, dance, and be silly with my grandchildren in person.

Then "The Poppie Show" will be canceled, which will be all right with me. Being a hands-on grandfather beats being a TV star any day.

CHAPTER 5

(For Sue and me, trying to get the coronavirus vaccine was like trying to get an audience with the pope. Fortunately, our daughters came to the rescue by going online and scheduling our shots. The question was: Could I get beer, too?)

"A Shot in the Dark"

After weeks of trying to get the coronavirus vaccine, during which Sue and I spent almost all of our waking hours online, on the phone, or on edge, I am happy and utterly flabbergasted to announce that our efforts were worth a shot, even though we haven't gotten it yet.

That's because we finally got appointments for our initial injections. And we owe it all to Katie and Lauren, who had been needling us (sorry, but it's true) to keep at it.

Ultimately, after realizing their parents were either unlucky or incompetent, they signed us up themselves.

The real reason we were unable to get appointments for so long is because we live in New York, a state that had been a global hot spot for the virus and then became a model for how to deal with it, but which now, in arranging vaccine distribution, is a total shot show.

Sue and I began our interminable search for an appointment when we registered on the state's COVID-19 website. Because we don't have any underlying conditions (we soon developed overlying conditions that included raging headaches, jittery nerves, and intestinal spasms that could be calmed only with over-the-counter medications such as wine), we were not in the first group of people eligible for the vaccine.

We were classified as 1b, which initially included people seventy-five and older but which was lowered for those sixty-five and up.

"1b or not 1b? That is the question," I told Sue.

"Here's the answer," she said. "We're both sixty-seven, so we qualify."

We thus embarked on our long day's journey into night, getting up with the chickens (the only ones we have are in the freezer) and staying up to the witching hour (or something that rhymes with it) just to see if we could get appointments on the state website.

We also called the "special" hotline number, which turned out to be a cold line because Sue once got a person who said, essentially, that it would be a cold day in hell before we got vaccinated.

"Good luck!" the woman said before hanging up.

The rest of the time, we were directed to the state website, where we had to reinsert our registration information only to find out that no appointments were available at any of the sites in our area.

The only two places in New York State where appointments were available were hundreds of miles away, both near the Canadian border.

"It might be easier to renew our passports and get vaccinated in Canada, eh!" I said with a horrible French-Canadian accent.

Sue shook her head. That was my reaction, too, when I cleverly figured out that even if we got appointments at one of those upstate sites, they might not be on the same day, which would involve two long round trips, and we'd have to go back for our second shots, which would involve two more.

So we registered with two national pharmacy chains where, of course, no appointments were available because they didn't even have vaccines.

In the meantime, Katie and Lauren kept telling us to go back on the state and pharmacy websites every day, all day, stopping only to eat or go to the bathroom, and constantly click, even after seeing that no appointments were available, in case something opened up.

Two things became disturbingly clear: (a) we were in grave danger of getting carpal tunnel syndrome and (b) the pandemic would be over before we got vaccinated.

Then, miraculously, on the same day, Katie and Lauren, who had been searching, too, got appointments for us. They are right around the corner at Stony Brook University.

Sue and I are grateful to our daughters for helping us get our first shots, which will be given soon.

Until then, we are celebrating with shots of our own: blackberry brandy for me, cinnamon whiskey for Sue.

And we don't even need an appointment.

"A Hello to Arms"

In an impressive act of bravery, I stood six feet away and, while wearing a bright red face mask that made my nose itch, watched Sue get her first coronavirus shot. As I will happily tell Dr. Anthony Fauci when he calls to congratulate me, I didn't even faint.

Of course, Sue deserves credit, too, because she suffered no ill effects aside from a headache that was probably caused by me. But it was just the first step in my superhuman fight to eradicate the virus. And it won't end until Sue and I have had both of our shots.

My first one will happen soon, but it was a long time coming because it took weeks for us to get appointments. And they wouldn't have happened without the help of Katie and Lauren, who went online and got us registered.

Our longtime friend Tim Lovelette knows the feeling: His older son, Marshall, got appointments for him and his wife, Jane.

"That's why God gave us kids — to keep us alive," Tim said. "Otherwise, we would have been dead long ago."

Tim and Jane got their first shots in an abandoned Circuit City building on Cape Cod, Massachusetts.

"It went smooth as silk," Tim reported. "And we both feel fine."

Hank Richert, another longtime friend, had an even better experience: He and his wife, Angela, who live in the Carolinas, have already gotten both of their shots. And they were given, of all places, at the Charlotte Motor Speedway.

"We made it to the finish line," Hank joked.

And he didn't need help from either of his sons to get appointments.

"Our medical group set it up for us," said Hank, who has a Ford Mustang GT convertible but instead drove his Hyundai Santa Fe to the speedway.

"We actually got to drive on the racetrack," Hank recalled. "They funneled us into a garage where race cars are serviced. We got to a station, rolled down the window, handed over our paperwork, stuck out our arms, and got our shots. That was the first time. I had a shot on a Saturday evening and Angela had hers the next morning. The second time, we got our shots on the same day. It was easy-peasy."

"Did they wave the checkered flag when you left?" I asked.

"No," answered Hank, who said he and Angela felt fine after both shots, "but it would have been a nice touch."

On the morning of Sue's initial injection, I revved up my Hyundai Santa Fe, an SUV that in this case stood for Shot Utility Vehicle, and drove to Stony Brook University.

We pulled up to a spot where a police officer sat in her patrol car.

"My wife has an appointment for a vaccine," I said, pointing to Sue.

"Hello, wife!" the cop chirped. Then she told me what to do: "Make a U-turn, go to the end of the road, turn right, and follow the signs."

"You're a cop and you just told me to make a U-turn?" I said incredulously.

"It's legal," she assured me. "And you won't go over a double yellow line, so I can't give you a ticket."

When I got to the second spot, another cop told me to follow the road and added, "Watch out for potholes."

"I bet Hank and Angela didn't have to do that at the speedway," I told Sue.

We parked the car and walked into the building where vaccines were being given. About ten minutes later, we arrived at a station where Sue turned over her paperwork, rolled up her sleeve, and got her shot.

"It was easy," she said afterward. "Everything was well-organized. And I didn't feel a thing. Next," she added, "it's your turn."

When it is, I'll know just what to say: "Paging Dr. Fauci!"

"A Shot and a Beer"

For anyone who is nervous about getting the coronavirus vaccine, I will allay your fears by saying that I got my first injection and suffered no ill effects aside from the lightheadedness I have had since birth.

On the negative side, you can't, no matter how hard you try, get a shot and a beer.

I found this out when I went to Stony Brook University and saw many helpful volunteers, security officials, and health care professionals but not, unfortunately, a bartender.

Of course, the fact that it was 9:30 in the morning may have had something to do with it.

I got the idea to ask for a cold one from my buddy Tim Lovelette, who said that when he got his first shot, he asked if he could have a brew, too.

"I said, 'Where's my beer?' They were giving me a shot and I even offered to pay for the beer, but they wouldn't give it to me," Tim said. "For my second shot, I'll bring my own."

I should have thought of that when I went for my first one, although Sue, who got her first shot ten days earlier and accompanied me for moral support, would have said that I was being even more ridiculous than usual.

When we pulled up to a spot where a cop was directing traffic for people with appointments, I said, "I brought my wife in case I pass out."

He nodded and said, "Good idea."

We parked the car and walked into the building where shots were being given.

A young woman put a digital thermometer to my forehead to take my temperature.

"Is my head empty?" I asked.

"I don't think so," she replied.

"Obviously, this isn't an X-ray machine," I said and moved on to a table where I had to show my paperwork. After that, Sue and I walked down a corridor and met a volunteer who asked, "Is this your first shot?"

"It's my ninth," I responded.

"Wow," she said. "You'll really be protected."

We moved on to another table and met Elana, who asked if I am allergic to anything.

"Only to myself," I answered.

"You're a standup comic," Elana said.

"If I sit down," I told her, "no one can see me."

"But we can still hear him," Sue chimed in.

"Can I get a shot and a beer?" I asked.

"No," Elana said. "It's a bit too early for beer, but some people have a little whiskey to calm their nerves."

"Are guys wimps when it comes to needles?" I wondered.

"We all know that," Elana replied. "But don't worry, this will be painless."

She was right, as I found out when I met Tina, who would be giving me an injection.

"How old are you?" she asked.

"Old enough to know better," I said. "But if you must know, I'm sixty-seven."

"You look great," Tina said. "What's your secret?"

"I eat like a horse, drink like a fish, and get absolutely no exercise," I said. "That's all there is to it."

"In which arm do you want me to give you a shot?" Tina asked.

"It doesn't matter," I said. "I'm ambidextrous. I'm incompetent with both."

"Pick one," she said.

"My left," I said as I rolled up my sleeve. "It's a good thing I'm not an octopus or I'd never make up my mind."

It was over in a flash.

"It didn't hurt," I said.

"Of course not," Tina replied.

"Can I get a beer?" I asked.

"Of course not," Tina replied again.

It figured. Still, I felt so good about getting my first shot that I went home with Sue and relaxed before having lunch. Afterward, I celebrated with a beer. It really hit the spot.

"On Puns and Needles"

Now that I have gotten my second dose of the coronavirus vaccine and am suffering no ill effects, aside from a troublesome bout of incoherence, which I was actually born with, I can say without fear of contradiction or incarceration that the pandemic is finally over.

Or more accurately, according to the nice and knowledgeable person who gave me the shot, it will likely end soon, thanks to my heroic and entirely questionable efforts.

I did my part to eradicate this once-in-a-century scourge by going with Sue, who had already received her second shot and accompanied me in case I fainted, to Stony Brook University, a major vaccination site with every important medical feature except, unfortunately, an open bar.

As I did the first time, I drove to the building that served as vaccine central. After Sue and I walked in and had our temperatures taken, I was directed to a table where a pleasant staffer named Charles asked to see my paperwork.

"Because I'm getting my second dose," I said, "does that mean the pandemic is over?"

"I hope so," Charles responded.

Tiffany, who sat next to him, added, "Now I don't have to get my second one."

"I'm here to help," I told her.

"I appreciate it," she said.

"I figured you were going in alphabetical order," I said. "And since my last name begins with a Z, this is the end of the virus."

"That explains why people are clearing out," Tiffany said.

"They probably saw me coming," I said. "I have that effect."

"I've heard that about you," Tiffany said as Charles handed me my paperwork and, very politely, told me where to go.

I walked down a hallway with Sue to a door with a sign that read: "Second shots."

We stood in line for about five minutes before I was directed to a station where Olivia would be giving me the vaccine.

"How did you react to your first shot?" she asked.

"Just fine," I said. "I liked it so much, I came back for a second one."

"Maybe you could come back for a third," Olivia suggested.

"I'd come back for a fifth," I replied, "but you don't serve alcohol, do you?"

"No, but I will rub alcohol on your arm before I give you the injection," answered Olivia.

"I've heard that some people get bad reactions to their second shots," I said.

"You might have a sore arm," Olivia said.

"Does this mean I won't be able to pitch in the major leagues?" I asked.

"I'm afraid so," she replied. "You might also have a fever and chills."

"Then I'd be running hot and cold," I noted.

"Any other concerns?" Olivia inquired.

"I'm naturally lightheaded, so how will I know the difference?" I wondered. "And what if I become incoherent?"

"Then your wife will ignore you," Olivia said.

Sue, who was standing nearby, nodded and said, "I do that anyway."

"Your wife is smart," Olivia said.

"You have a point," I noted.

"Actually, I do," said Olivia, who used it to painlessly give me the shot.

"Do you realize," I said as I buttoned my shirt and took a card signifying I was fully vaccinated, "that when the pandemic is over, the only people wearing masks will be bank robbers?"

"Until then," Olivia said, "you should still wear one when you go out. But you are doing your part to eradicate the virus."

"So far, it's kept me off the streets," I said. "But pretty soon, I'll be on the loose again. And no one will be safe from my stupid jokes."

"In that case," Olivia said, "people may have to be vaccinated against you."

CHAPTER 6

(Free at last! Fully vaccinated, Sue and I could start to see people again. That includes the grandkids and my mother. Was the long wait worth it? What do you think?)

"Put on a Happy Face"

The problem with wearing a mask — aside from the lamentable fact that you can't breathe, talk, or make funny faces — is that no one can see you smile.

Not that there has been much to smile about over the past year. The pandemic has forced everyone to wear a mask, the result being that I couldn't see people smile at my frustrating inability to make funny faces or tell stupid jokes.

But I dropped the mug rug when, after receiving my second coronavirus vaccine, I saw Chloe and Lilly for the first time in months without having to wear a mask.

"Poppie!" they squealed in unison when I walked in the front door of their house to watch them while Lauren ran errands.

They still recognized me. I think the mustache was a giveaway because Sue, known to our five grandchildren as Nini, doesn't have one.

Sue and I had seen Chloe and Lilly the previous day for an afternoon of outdoor fun and frolic, the first time we had done so maskless in I can't remember how long. (I can't remember because wearing a mask every day has cut off the air supply to what little remains of my brain.)

At any rate, the only way our grandchildren could see us since this whole viral business began is on FaceTime, which has given me a chance to show my Face one silly session at a Time.

But now, I was finally resuming my cherished role as The Manny, a big-baby babysitter whose grandkids are more mature than I am.

"Where's your mask, Poppie?" asked Chloe, who just turned eight.

"In the car," I replied.

"You look better without it," said Lilly, who's four.

Then, announcing she was the Tooth Fairy, Lilly handed me a small mesh candy bag with forty cents in it.

"You deserve it, Poppie," Lilly said. "You lost your buck teef when you were little. I didn't lose my buck teef," which she couldn't pronounce without, of course, her "buck teef."

As the three of us used all of our teeth to eat lunch — mac and cheese — it dawned on me that Chloe and Lilly may be the only people on earth happy to see my full visage again.

Afterward, we went outside to the girls' picnic table, which served as Lilly's Restaurant, where I was served a dessert of freshly picked flowers.

"Yummy!" I exclaimed as I pretended to munch on the delicious dandelions, which I pretended to wash down with dandelion wine.

"You don't have to wear your mask in my restaurant," Lilly informed me.

After running around the yard and playing on the swings, we went back inside, where Lilly changed into her Princess Aurora costume from "Sleeping Beauty."

"Would you like me to change into a costume?" I asked, which prompted Lilly's resounding response: "No!"

Chloe got on her FreeTime to show me "Hello Kitty Discovering the World."

"Let's go to Australia!" she said.

"Do I need a passport?" I wondered.

"Of course not, silly Poppie!" Chloe answered.

After visiting all the continents, I made a mental note to put in for mileage on my tax returns.

Then the girls climbed into my lap so I could read "Paulette: The Pinkest Puppy in the World."

"She's having a ruff day!" Chloe joked.

It was a wonderful visit, especially since we could actually hear each other.

"Do you know what you sound like with a mask on?" Chloe asked.

"What?" I replied.

"Um, um, um!" Chloe said.

"Ugh, ugh, ugh!" Lilly joined in.

We all laughed. When Lauren got back, it was time to leave.

Without a mask on, it was easy to show the girls I had a great time. They could see it from a smile away.

"Mother and (Grown-up) Child Reunion"

I was born more than three weeks past my due date, an act of monumental tardiness that kept my mother waiting for nearly ten months to give birth to an eight-pound, thirteen-ounce baby who is even larger now but, sadly, no more mature.

But that was nothing (easy for me to say because I have not, as yet, given birth) compared to the fifteen months my mother, Rosina, had to wait to see me after the pandemic struck.

Now that we have been vaccinated, it was safe for me to venture back to my hometown of Stamford, Connecticut, to visit my mom, who at ninety-six is in better shape than I am, both physically (except for her sore knees, which will probably sideline her for the remainder of the baseball season) and mentally (so are hanging plants, one of which I brought to her as a gift).

I pulled my car into the driveway and was enthusiastically greeted by my sister Elizabeth's sweet pooch, Lucie, who is fourteen and, in dog years, is as old as my mother and almost as frisky.

"Woof, Woof!" (translation: "Hi, Lucie!") I exclaimed as the cuddly canine planted a kiss on my kisser.

"I think you're barking up the wrong tree," said my sister Susan, who with Elizabeth lives with our mom and helps take care of her.

We both laughed and hugged for the first time since January 2020.

Susan, Lucie, and I went inside and waited for my mother to come downstairs from her bedroom, where she was getting dolled up for my appearance.

About fifteen minutes later, I heard the sound of the stairlift, a contraption my mother calls "my magic carpet," delivering her to the front hallway, which is next to the family room, where Susan and I were sitting.

My mother rolled into the room with the help of her rollator and said from behind me, "Hello, stranger!"

I turned around and, with mock indignation, huffed, "Can't you see I'm talking with Susan?"

I turned back around and pretended to continue the conversation with my sister.

There was a moment of silence before we all burst into laughter. I got up and embraced my mother, who hugged me so tightly that she almost cracked my ribs. As a retired nurse, she could have fixed me up in a jiffy.

"I've waited for fifteen months for this day," my mother said when she finally released me.

"That's even longer than you waited for me to be born," I noted.

"And look what I got," my mother joked.

What she got was a son who inherited her sense of humor, if not her punctuality. In fact, my mother is always joking, which in recent years has helped her bounce back from broken bones (leg, wrist, and back) as well as a bump to the head, which, she said, "is too hard to break."

Since it was raining, we couldn't go outside, which was fine with me because the week before, my mother was visited by a bear.

"It came out of the woods and snapped two metal plant hooks like they were twigs," my mother said.

"You could have scared it away with your trusty BB gun," I said, referring to the air pistol my mom uses for — no kidding — target practice in the backyard.

"That makes you a son of a gun," she quipped.

When Elizabeth came home, we hugged and laughed when I told her about the greeting I got from Lucie.

"She loves her Uncle Jerry," Elizabeth said.

Susan's son Blair, a wonderfully enterprising young man who also lives in the house, walked in wearing his "magnetic hat," a baseball cap on which he attached magnets that hold some of the small tools he uses at work.

"That's using your head!" I told him.

We sent out for pizza and had a laugh-filled dinner before I left for home.

"This has been one of the best days of my life," my mother said as she gave me another hug. "And just like when you were born, it was worth the wait."

"The Cult of Poppie"

After a year and a half, which was how long it had been since I had seen my twin grandchildren, I can finally say, with great pride in my corruptive influence as a silly grandfather, that the toddlers have joined my other three grandkids in the Cult of Poppie.

This was one of the highlights of the recent visit Sue and I paid to Katie and her family: husband Dave; older son Xavier, who is four; and the dynamic duo, Zoe and her younger (by twenty-five minutes) brother, Quinn, who will turn two next month.

The twins were only five months old the last time Sue and I saw them in person and had not yet fallen under my spell. But they are now full-fledged fans, along with Xavier and our oldest two grandchildren, Chloe, eight, and Lilly, four and a half, who are the daughters of Lauren and Guillaume.

Because all the adults in the family have been vaccinated, it was safe for Sue and me to drive to Washington, D.C., to be reunited with Katie's clan.

After sharing hugs and kisses with Katie, we drove a few blocks to get Xavier at school. He also greeted us with hugs and kisses. It was like we picked up where we left off the last time we saw him, when he was only two and a half.

Even though the twins have often seen us on FaceTime, which has given me a marvelous opportunity to act stupid from a distance, they probably thought we were TV celebrities who stood only three inches tall. Katie warned us that Zoe, in particular, was skittish around unfamiliar people.

Those fears melted away a few minutes after we saw the kids back at Katie and Dave's house. Following an initial reticence, Quinn and, yes, Zoe opened up with smiles and giggles. They especially liked my shenanigans, marveling at the fact that I could act stupid in person, too.

I continued my foolishness the next day, when we all went to a park to celebrate the birthday of one of Xavier's friends. I chased Xavier and his pals around the playground, nearly collapsing in the broiling sun, then did kiddie lifting with Quinn and followed up by pushing Zoe on the swings.

Later, Dave and I cooled off with beer.

That frosty beverage also hit the spot the next day, when Dave and I took Xavier to Nationals Park to see the hometown Washington Nationals play their Beltway rivals, the Baltimore Orioles.

But first, Sue, Katie, and I took the twins to another park for morning soccer. It was athletic competition at its finest, coordinated by coach John Jenkins, who at the beginning of the season had named Zoe the captain of the group because, he told me, "She took my hand the first day, so I said, 'All right, she's the captain.' Zoe is our best player."

All the kids — except Quinn, who was off to the side, munching on a bag of Goldfish — paid attention as Coach Jenkins asked, "Do we touch the ball with our ears?"

"No!" the little stars responded.

"Our noses?"

"No!"

"Our hands?"

"No!"

"Our feet?"

"Yes!"

"Very good," said Coach Jenkins, who turned around and told the adults, "Nobody listens to me at home."

What followed wasn't exactly Olympic-caliber play, but it was entertaining. At the end, Quinn finally decided to participate, kicking a ball the length of the soccer area into a goal.

"Better late than never," Sue commented.

Chaos ensued, prompting Coach Jenkins to admit, "I see I'm losing control here."

We subsequently went to another area of the park, where the kids cheered a couple of sanitation workers as they loaded trash into their truck.

"Poppie makes messes and these gentlemen clean them up," I told the twins.

"I like that!" one of the guys exclaimed.

Zoe and Quinn also met Teddy, a one-hundred-and-fifty-pound Great Dane.

"He's even better than a Mediocre Dane," I said.

The big dog barked in approval.

In the afternoon, there was the baseball game, which Xavier thoroughly enjoyed, not so much for the action on the field, where the Nats prevailed, 6-5, but for the hot dog and ice cream that Poppie bought for him. In return, Dave bought me and himself the aforementioned frosty beverages.

Katie, Xavier, Zoe, Quinn, Sue, and I went to the zoo the next day. Xavier liked seeing an alligator that had just its eyes sticking up above the surface of its mossy pool and the twins enjoyed seeing a massively tusked elephant throw dirt on itself.

We also saw an otter, which prompted me to ask, "Where's the otter one?"

A couple of fellow grandparents chortled. One of them said, "The otter one? Very good!"

After a sea lion got my seal of approval, Xavier said, "I'm finished."

"Me, too," I said. "This place is a real zoo."

The following day, Katie, the three kids, Sue, and I went to West Potomac Park, where Xavier and I had a riverside picnic.

"There must be a lot of fish in the water," I said.

"What about sharks?" he asked.

"I don't know, but what other creatures do you think are in there?" I asked.

"Maybe crabs," Xavier replied.

"How about worms?" I wondered.

Xavier stopped eating his cheese puffs, looked over at me, and said, politely but firmly, "Worms live underground, Poppie."

Still, I managed to worm my way into the affections of all three children. I also managed to see a good deal of Washington, including the aquatic gardens, the arboretum, the art museum, and, from a distance, the Capitol.

In our week there, I also saw approximately one thousand three hundred and eighty-seven cicadas, five of which were still alive.

All in all, Sue and I had a wonderful visit. It was a long time coming but well worth the wait.

On the last day, we hugged and kissed Katie, Dave, and the kids, who didn't want us to go. By that time, the twins were completely converted.

"You'll be happy to know," Katie told me, "that Zoe and Quinn have officially joined the Cult of Poppie."

"Poppie at the Bat"

If, as a former sportswriter, I could vote for players to be inducted into the Baseball Hall of Fame, I would cast ballots for a pair of superstars who deserve to have plaques alongside the greats of our national pastime.

I refer, of course, to Chloe and Lilly.

The girls showed off their hitting and pitching prowess during the first sleepover they have had at my house since last year.

Our activities, most of which also involved Sue, included baking cookies, eating pancakes, drawing pictures, watching movies ("Zombies" and "Zombies 2"), going out for ice cream, riding in a kiddie car, zooming down a slide, blowing bubbles, and — the highlight of the visit — playing Wiffle ball.

One player who definitely won't get into the Hall of Fame (unless he buys a ticket) is yours truly, who proved to be even worse at playing sports than I was at writing about them.

That was sadly evident when the girls and I set up a Wiffle ball field in the backyard, where they clobbered my pitches and made me whiff at theirs.

But first, we had to have spring training, which entailed showing the girls how to hold the plastic bat.

"Are you a righty or a lefty?" I asked Chloe, who held the bat on her left shoulder but with her hands transposed.

"OK," I said after I had corrected her grip. When Chloe stood facing me, I said, "Turn a bit, hold the bat up, look over your right shoulder, and watch the ball."

Two seconds later, after making an underhand pitch, I watched the ball rocket past my head.

"Good hit, Chloe!" yelled Lilly, who picked up the ball and, with her right hand, threw it back to me on the fly.

"Good throw, Lilly!" I said.

"Thank you, Poppie," Lilly replied modestly. "Can I hit?"

"Let's give Chloe a few more chances," I said.

My next pitch was low. Chloe didn't swing.

"Good eye," I commented.

Chloe fouled off the next pitch, which was inside. She chased an outside toss before digging in.

"Two strikes," I said. "One more and you're out."

My next pitch was down the middle. Chloe parked it. In fact, the exit velocity must have exceeded the speed at which cars blow through the stop sign in front of the house.

"Home run!" I exclaimed.

"My turn!" said Lilly, also a lefty with whom I had to go through the same routine: hand placement, correct stance, raised bat, watchful eye.

She pulled my first pitch down the line for what would have been a ground-rule double.

"Nice hit, Lilly!" yelled Chloe.

Lilly missed the next two pitches.

"One more?" she asked as I went into my windup.

The word "yes" was barely out of my mouth when Lilly's batted ball almost hit me in the mouth.

"Home run!" Lilly declared.

If I had been the starting pitcher in a major league game, I would have been sent to the showers. So I decided it was my turn to bat.

Chloe was the relief pitcher. Her first toss was low, but I swung anyway — and missed.

"Strike one!" Lilly yelled from what passed for the outfield.

Unfortunately, I never got the ball out of the infield. Chloe's baffling assortment of pitches sent me down on strikes.

Then Lilly came in to pitch. The result was pretty much the same, although I did foul off a couple of pitches and actually hit one, but it went directly to Chloe, who scooped it up and tagged me.

When the game was called on account of pain (I hurt my knee), Chloe and Lilly had made a strong case for induction into the Baseball Hall of Fame.

As for me, being sent down to the minors was the only option after being beaten by a couple of minors.

And the poet who penned "Casey at the Bat" might have concluded: "But there is no joy in Oldville — mighty Poppie has struck out."

"The Macaroni Man"

If I were to write a book about my adventures in Italian cooking — the highlight being a dish called Zezima's Zesty Ziti Zinger, which did not, I will say for legal purposes, kill legendary actor Paul Newman — I would title it "Remembrance of Things Pasta."

And the *pièce de résistance* (a French phrase meaning "resist a piece of anything I make") would be my delicious homemade linguine.

Actually, I only had a hand — and a messy one at that — in a macaroni marathon that included my mother, Rosina; my sister Susan; and Susan's adult children, Taylor, Blair, and Whitney.

All of us contributed to a meal for the ages, the greatest age (ninety-six) being that of my mother. Even now, she's a kitchen magician who was inspired by her late mother, affectionately known as Nana, who began the family tradition of making pasta from scratch.

One of my remembrances was when my sister Elizabeth, then just a kid, sneaked into my bedroom and scrunched up strips of uncooked macaroni that Nana had carefully laid out on a large cloth on the bed.

Elizabeth wasn't sent to bed without dinner, which I also remember as being delicious, but she must have learned her lesson because she resisted the urge to scrunch up strips of uncooked macaroni at the recent culinary confab.

One family member who was not known for his pasta prowess — or his cooking skill at all, unless you count toast or boiled water — was my late father, the original and best Jerry Zezima, who nonetheless was famous for his salads and often made a great dish of macaroni (from a box) with oil and garlic.

I got my skill (or lack thereof) from him — with the exception of my one gastronomic triumph: About twenty years ago, I created Zezima's Zesty Ziti Zinger, for which I was first runner-up in the pasta sauce division of the Newman's Own and Good Housekeeping Recipe Contest, a national competition that featured thousands of entries.

Before I brought a dish of the stuff to New York City for Paul Newman to try, I fed some to my dog, Lizzie, who wolfed it down and begged for more.

When I told Newman about the canine taste test, he asked, "Is your dog still alive?"

"Woof!" I replied, at which point his blue eyes sparkled. Then he dug in and wolfed the stuff down himself.

On the advice of my attorney, I am obligated to say that Newman's death several years later cannot be attributed to food poisoning.

And I am happy to report that everyone survived my admittedly modest contribution to the homemade pasta dinner that was created in my mother's kitchen.

The enthusiastic eaters included Taylor's wife, Carlin; Elizabeth, an excellent cook who sat this one out, and her sweet pooch, Lucie, who was more than willing to wolf down a dish but had to settle for a bowl of dog food.

My mother started the macaroni making by pouring flour onto a large board on the counter and creating a powdery circle. Then she cracked two eggs, plopped the yolks and whites into the center, added a pinch each of black pepper and nutmeg, and used her fingers to slowly and carefully mix it all together until it was a softball-sized mound that she continued to knead until the consistency was just right.

Next it was Whitney's turn and she did a terrific job.

"I need to knead," I declared.

So I stepped up to the counter and, with all eyes on me, poured the flour, cracked the eggs, added the pepper and nutmeg, and proceeded to make a gooey lump that looked like spackle.

With the help of Whitney, who was Julia Child by comparison, and Susan, a wonderful cook who had made the sauce (we call it gravy) and fried up a bunch of meatballs and sausages, I finally got my dough ball mixed well enough that it didn't have to be used in a bocce tournament.

Taylor and Blair, the Boyz n the Range Hood, showed brotherly love by running all the dough balls through an attachment on my mother's Mixmaster to make the strips of linguine that Susan and Blair boiled and we all avidly consumed.

Afterward, my mother said to me, "You did a good job."

"Thanks," I replied. "Nana — and Paul Newman — would be proud."

"Granddaughters' Art Is a Big Draw"

As a painter, I like to think I have something in common with Picasso, mainly because we both had blue periods, mine coming when I used that color to paint the bathroom.

But I pale (my beige period, when I did the soffits in the kitchen) compared to Chloe and Lilly, who not only deserve to have a brush with fame, but whose talent is on full display in a watercolor show at my house, proving to critics and connoisseurs alike that home is where the art is.

I may not know a Manet from a Monet, except that their paintings cost a lot of Money, but I know what I like, which is why I have established Zezima's Two Rules of Modern Art.

Rule No. 1: If you see an artwork that's titled something like "Spring Butterfly," but it looks more like the grille of a '57 Chevy, don't buy it.

Rule No. 2: If an artist has been working on a piece for months and when it's finally finished he calls it "Untitled," it means even he doesn't know what it is. Don't buy that one, either.

But there's no mistaking what Chloe and Lilly have accomplished in their brief but brilliant careers.

The gallery at the Zezimanse, where the girls' paintings hang (or, rather, are taped to the family room wall), is their latest exhibit.

I witnessed the creation of these masterpieces when the girls had a sleepover and asked if they could paint.

I sat them in their usual spots at the kitchen table, spread out some newspapers (including copies of my columns, which have never been confused with art), got them their brushes and paint, plopped down a stack of white printer paper, filled two small plastic cups with water, and watched as the magic happened.

Chloe went to work on a rainbow. The bold yet delicate strokes were reminiscent of van Gogh, who definitely had an eye for beauty but not, unfortunately, an ear for it.

Lilly went for a more modern look, especially after she spilled the contents of her cup on the various shapes (circle, rectangle, blob) that began to run with all the hues in her palette, putting the water in watercolor.

But the girls don't work only with brushes. They also use pencils, crayons, and markers on their colorful creations.

These implements can be useless in the hands of a hack, as I found out when I used a marker to draw Shrimpy, a pink crustacean in one of the girls' favorite movies, "Zombies 2."

"It's not so good," I admitted.

"That's OK, Poppie," Chloe said. "You just need to practice."

I thought I would do better when Lilly, who had drawn "Anna," a girl with blue hair, yellow eyes, an apricot face, and mosquito bites on her chin, wanted me to draw a dress. I took a marker and outlined the garment.

"You put sleeves on the dress!" Lilly scolded. "I don't like sleeves! That's a bad dress!"

Then she showed me how to do it right by drawing a sleeveless dress, which she painted gold.

Chloe painted a wedding dress with a blue neckline, a pink waistline, and a red, orange, yellow, green, blue, purple, and pink hemline.

I tried drawing another dress, this one sans sleeves, but Lilly said, "It's still bad."

I had flunked Art 101, which explains why none of my pieces are in the show, which includes paintings of a unicorn, a butterfly, and a flower.

At least Sue has faith in my artistry. In fact, she wants me to paint the dining room. It looks like I'll be going back to my blue period.

"On With the Show"

When it comes to dancing, Chloe and Lilly have more talent in their pinky toes than I have in both of my size-eleven feet. And it doesn't help when I try to improve my fumbling footwork with something inspirational — like wine.

So it was fitting that the girls' recent recital, in which they were dancing stars, was held at a vineyard.

They didn't perform in the tap room, even though they had a couple of great tap routines, but they did wow an audience of about two hundred and fifty dance fans under a tent on the grounds of Peconic Bay Vineyards in Cutchogue, New York.

The show was put on by Inspire Dance Centre of Southold, New York, where the girls take lessons. And where I should, too.

"We have adult classes," said artistic director Meagan Grattan, known to the students as Miss Meagan.

"I can't cut a rug, so you'd have your work cut out for you," I told her.

But that could wait because the focus was on the performers — the best of whom, in my totally unbiased opinion, were Chloe and Lilly.

Of the eighteen dances on the program, they were in five — Chloe three and Lilly two.

The third act was "Dumbo the Flying Elephant," featuring the pre-K ballet class.

Lilly led the way, prancing out on the large stage and standing at the far left in the front row. She smiled and waved to acknowledge the smiles and waves of me, Sue, Lauren, and Guillaume. We were seated on folding chairs about halfway back in the tent.

My main contribution to the show was to giggle, clap, and exclaim, "That was great!" I got what I hoped were appreciative looks from the people around us.

I certainly appreciated Lilly's performance, in which she crossed her arms and swiveled her hips to the beat of the song "Baby Mine." She grinned broadly as the class exited the stage to a big ovation.

Chloe starred in the eighth routine, "Magic Carpet Ride," featuring the first- and second-grade ballet. She sat cross-legged in front, then got up and showed off perfect jumps and fluid foot movement to the strains of "A Whole New World" from "Aladdin." Chloe flashed a big smile at the end and, with the other girls, got an enthusiastic round of applause.

"Oh, man, that was wonderful!" I chirped.

A young mother in the row in front of us turned around and smiled.

Chloe came out again in the twelfth act, "Journey of the Little Mermaid," with the first- and second-grade tap class. To the strains of "Under the Sea," she moved flawlessly, from left to right in the front row, then to the back, and finished up in front again. The choreography was terrific. Chloe smiled as she and the other girls exited the stage, making way for the next routine, which featured Lilly.

She was the most animated performer in "The Seas With Nemo and Friends," featuring the pre-K tap class. Lilly flashed a big smile when we waved to her at the beginning of the song "Just Keep Swimming." She just kept dancing until the song was over and waved as she left the stage.

Three routines later, Chloe came out with the first- and second-grade jazz group to perform "Splash Mountain," featuring the song "Zip-A-Dee-Doo-Dah." My, oh my, what a wonderful dance! Chloe did perfect leg lifts, jumps, and arm lifts, exiting with hands on hips in the big finish, waving and smiling as she went off.

At the show's end, Chloe and Lilly were presented with flowers from Lauren and Guillaume and from me and Sue. They posed for pictures and said they had a great time. Then we all went to the vineyard and sat at a table outside so the girls could eat chips and the adults could savor refreshments.

"This wine makes me feel like dancing!" I remarked.

"Please," Sue said, "stay seated."

Later, Miss Meagan told me that Chloe and Lilly were among her best students.

"Maybe they can be on 'America's Got Talent' and wow Simon Cowell," I said.

"You never know!" Miss Meagan replied.

"Should they get an agent?" I asked.

"Chloe for sure," she said. "Lilly will be Chloe's agent. Chloe knows all the routines and Lilly is the line leader. They even correct my mistakes."

"What about me?" I wondered.

"You could be in our adult tap class," Miss Meagan suggested. "We have a few ladies who are retired. They danced when they were younger and want to get back into it."

"To me, a tap involves beer," I said. "Or wine. Which wouldn't help me dance better. I bet Simon Cowell would agree."

"In the Pink (and Purple) at the Spa"

I may not be as tough as nails, but my nails are tough. And colorful. And I owe it all to the talented cosmetologists at Lilly & Chloe's House of Beauty.

Lilly and Chloe happen to be my granddaughters. And the house where they made me beautiful is the one I live in with Sue, who also is beautiful but was about to go out when the girls, who were visiting for the day, asked if they could paint their nails.

Sue and Lauren, the little beauticians' beautiful mommy, were going shopping. Lauren's handsome husband, Guillaume, the girls' daddy, was going out, too.

I was in charge. And I ended up getting my nails painted — at no charge.

Let me tell you, it was worth every penny.

The spa opened in the kitchen, where Lilly, Chloe, and yours truly sat at the table with a couple of bottles of nail polish — one pink, the other purple — which Sue got for them from an upstairs bathroom, one of the many spots in the house where beauty products (none belonging to me) are kept.

"Be good for Poppie," Sue told the girls before she and Lauren left. "And don't make a mess."

It was an ominous warning.

As soon as the door closed, Chloe asked me to paint her fingernails purple to match her dress.

"Let me show you how," said Chloe, who at eight years old is a veteran of the cosmetological arts. Then she started painting the nails of her left hand.

Lilly, meanwhile, sat at the table with the bottle of pink polish in front of her.

"Don't do anything until Chloe and I are done," I said.

"OK, Poppie," said Lilly, who is four and a half but already has a keen interest in beauty. That includes diamonds. Her poor parents.

Anyway, Chloe painted her nails perfectly. Since she is right-handed, she didn't want to use her left hand to paint the nails of her right hand. So I became her right-hand man. This may be a left-handed compliment, but I did a good job.

I knew it when Chloe said, "Good job, Poppie."

Suddenly, Lilly shrieked, "I spilled my nail polish!"

Sure enough, she got the pink stuff all over her blue dance outfit, which for some reason she was wearing over her regular clothes. She also was wearing a ton of costume jewelry — including, she informed me, a diamond ring.

I grabbed some paper towels and tried to get the polish off. I refrained, however, from using Windex.

When it was obvious that my efforts were hopeless, Lilly sat back down and said, "Now paint my nails, Poppie."

I did another good job.

"It's your turn," said Lilly, announcing that she was going to paint my fingernails.

She dipped a brush into the bottle of pink polish, or what was left of it, and smeared a gob onto my right thumbnail. I used a paper towel, or what was left of them, to wipe excess polish off the thumb itself.

Then Lilly dipped a brush into the bottle of purple polish and painted the nail on my right index finger.

She alternated colors until I had a pink pinky.

"Now I'm going to do your left hand," said Lilly, who repeated the process, except that she started with purple on my thumbnail and ended with the same color on my pinky.

"You look beautiful, Poppie!" Lilly gushed.

"Good job, Lilly!" declared Chloe, who went upstairs to give herself a beauty treatment with Sue's makeup.

When Sue and Lauren got home, they marveled at my colorful nails.

"Oh, my God!" Sue exclaimed.

"I can't believe this!" Lauren chimed in.

"What's the matter," I asked, "are you ladies jealous?"

Aside from failing to notice that Lilly's chair was covered in nail polish, not all of which came off, I had a wonderful day at the spa.

"Next time, Poppie," Lilly promised, "I'll paint your toenails."

"A Guy Who's Old Goes for the Gold"

I am all wet, even during droughts, which is why I am sorry that the Summer Olympics don't have a Slip 'N Slide competition.

If they did, I'd be the favorite to bring home the gold for my dazzling performance on the watery plastic sheet, which impressed my granddaughters so much that they gave me perfect scores, after which I had to recuperate with a cold beer, the drink of champions.

I trained for this high-stakes event — which wasn't televised but did stream, so to speak, on a cellphone — with Chloe and Lilly, superior athletes who humiliated me in other water-related competitions.

One was the Super Soaker, which required me to lumber across the backyard to their inflatable pool, jump in without spraining an ankle or rupturing a vital organ, grab a pressurized water gun, and engage in a marksmanship battle with the girls, who hit the bull's-eye (me) so often that I looked like I had been through a monsoon.

Another was 1-2-3 Sunshine, a game in which I had to sneak up on either Chloe or Lilly (or both) before they turned around and sprayed me with a hose. I was disqualified every time. I just stood there, utterly defeated, as water poured off me like Niagara Falls.

The only contest at which I excelled — though not without injury — was on the Slip 'N Slide, which stretched fifteen feet on a slight downward slope and was kept constantly slippery by water that sprinkled out of one side, providing a steady shower through which I thumped, bumped, and slid, sometimes out of control and often with painful results.

The girls had already shown fine form in this challenging event, though Lilly went about two feet on her stomach before deciding that sliding on her knees was the better option. She got the hang of it after a couple of tries.

Chloe did the knee slide about halfway down on her initial run before covering the entire course the next time.

Then it was my turn.

"Come on, Poppie!" Chloe exhorted.

"You can do it!" shouted Lilly.

I was understandably nervous as I imagined that I was in the Olympic spotlight, TV cameras trained on my flabby physique while the announcers wondered how, at sixty-seven, I had ever made the U.S. team and whether the gold medal, if I actually won, would have to be presented to me in a hospital.

The rules, according to the girls, stated that I had to slide on my stomach, not my knees. This entailed getting a running start and flopping down on my belly, which made me worry that I would miscalculate the landing and end up sounding like a mezzo-soprano.

My worries washed away as I executed a perfect flop and slid flawlessly down the narrow strip to the finish line in what must have been world record time.

"Awesome!" Chloe exclaimed.

"Yeah!" Lilly chimed in.

Sue and Lauren witnessed my performance from a nearby table, where they were sipping wine and hoping they wouldn't have to perform CPR.

"Go again, Poppie!" Chloe urged.

I outdid myself with an even better run. I went several more times, whooshing my way to athletic glory.

I must admit that I suffered plastic burns on my stomach and knees. But, like the champ I am, I shook it off and celebrated with a beer.

"How did I do?" I asked the girls, telling them to rate me on a scale of 1 to 10.

"You got a 10!" Chloe said, giving me the thumbs-up.

"I give you 189," Lilly added. "Plus 50."

No offense to U.S. swim team stars Katie Ledecky and Caeleb Dressel, but even they couldn't have beaten me had the Olympic committee seen fit to add Slip 'N Slide to this year's competition.

But that, as Chloe and Lilly might say, is water under the grandfather.

CHAPTER 7

(Laughter is the best medicine, especially for baby boomers who want to stay healthy. That's why seeing a physician for various ailments is just what the doctor ordered. But joining a gym? It's a stretch.)

"It's a Mad, Mad, Mad, Mad Tooth"

When it comes to mad scientists, there was no one madder than the Invisible Man, whose Hollywood smile couldn't be seen because, of course, he was wearing invisible braces.

I have a Hollywood smile because I have been wearing invisible braces for several years. So when one of my two retainers cracked, which was probably the result of a wisecrack, I watched as Dr. Max Sanacore, who isn't a mad scientist (otherwise, he'd be known as Mad Max) but does work in a laboratory, made me a new one.

Actually, Dr. Max is in his last year at the Stony Brook University School of Dental Medicine, where he is the latest in a string of student orthodontists who have made sure that my pearly whites stay on the straight and narrow.

The root (see: wisecrack, above) of the problem was that my right upper lateral incisor began to rotate like the tires on my car. Fortunately, I didn't have to go to a mechanic. To compound matters, my left central lower incisor started to look like the Leaning Tower of Pisa, the key difference being that tourists couldn't see it because I always had my foot in my mouth.

I went to Stony Brook and got invisible braces, a pair of clear plastic devices that slowly but effectively straightened my two wayward teeth. It was a lot better than getting the metal kind, which look like miniature railroad tracks and put beer drinkers like me in danger of being hit by flying refrigerator magnets.

After the bottom retainer split, without so much as a goodbye note, I went back to Stony Brook and saw Dr. Max.

"First," he said as I settled into the chair, "I have to make an impression."

"I think you're very impressive," I told him.

"Thanks," he said. "Now please open your mouth."

Peering into the oral equivalent of the Grand Canyon, Dr. Max filled a metal tray with alginate, a gooey substance that contains seaweed, which made me want to cry for kelp, and pressed it over my bottom teeth.

"Can you breathe?" he asked.

"Ong, ong, ong," I responded affirmatively.

For a full minute, I drooled with the force of Niagara Falls, which at my age happens with alarming frequency.

When the molar eclipse was over, Dr. Max took me into a back room that looked like a laboratory where a mad scientist might conduct a hideous experiment on an unsuspecting patient whose brain would be transplanted into the head of a gorilla.

Fortunately for apes everywhere, I don't have the kind of gray matter that could possibly do them any good. In fact, the gray matter that would become my new bottom retainer was being molded and heated by Dr. Max.

"You could train a monkey to do this," he said.

"Not with my brain," I replied.

Dr. Max, who has more than a smattering of smarts, originally studied engineering.

"On my last day of college, I said to myself, 'I don't want to be an engineer. I want to be a dentist.' So I came here," said Dr. Max, who's thirty and will graduate in June. "Then I'll have to get a real job," he added.

For now, he's doing great work, the most important being the creation of my new bottom retainer. He showed me how to pour the alginate, put it in a vibrating machine to get the air bubbles out, and heat it up in another machine so, he said, "it's nice and malleable." Then he trimmed it into shape.

Later that afternoon, the retainer was ready. I snapped it onto my bottom teeth.

"Perfect!" I exclaimed.

"Now you can keep your Hollywood smile," said Dr. Max.

"Thanks," I said. "The Invisible Man would be jealous."

"Dotting My Eye"

I spy with my swollen eye, which got that way because of a stye.

It may come as no surprise that when I took poetry in high school, I wasn't a very good pupil. That my pupil was covered by an inflamed eyelid was a big surprise to me, especially after Sue told me to put a hot teabag on the painful peeper and started calling me "Winky."

I became a double-visionary when I felt something — an eyelash, a piece of dirt, possibly a ham sandwich — in my left eye.

Wisely avoiding the temptation to use a metal rake to remove the ocular invader, I stuck a finger in my eye, though not in the same stern manner that Moe often poked Larry, Curly, or Shemp in order to disabuse his fellow Stooges from abusing him.

It didn't work. So I tried flooding my eye with shower water. That only compounded the problem. So did an inadvertent squirting of soap, which burned like hell.

A couple of days later, my left eyelid had ballooned to the size of — you guessed it — a balloon, though without "Happy birthday!" written on it.

My lid was so red that if I had stood on a street corner, cars may actually have stopped.

"What's going on, Winky?" Sue asked cheerily.

"My eyelid is about to erupt like Mount St. Helens," I grumbled.

"You have a stye," she informed me. "Put a hot teabag on it."

Sue should know, not only because she has had this ailment herself, but because she drinks approximately half the world's supply of tea. If she saved a year's worth of bags, they would be piled as high as the Empire State Building.

I boiled some water, poured it in a cup, dunked in a teabag, pressed it to my eyelid, and let out a scream that rattled the windows.

"You have to make the teabag as hot as you can stand it," Sue said.

"That's all I can stand," I replied, echoing Popeye. "I can't stands no more."

So I went to a walk-in clinic and saw Dr. Lindsey Schuster, who asked if I use glasses.

"Only those that hold wine or beer," I responded.

"You have a stye," she said before prescribing an antibiotic ointment. "If it doesn't work, you should see an eye doctor."

The ointment didn't work, so I went to see Dr. Howard Weinberg.

"You have a stye," he said.

"My wife told me to put a hot teabag on it," I told him.

"What happened?" Dr. Weinberg wondered.

"It scalded my eyelid," I reported. "And the caffeine kept my eye open all night."

"I've seen a lot more styes lately," he said. "They're caused by the face masks people wear. Their breath goes into their eyes."

"What if they have bad breath?" I asked.

"Then," Dr. Weinberg answered, "they'll get stink eye."

"What can I do to get rid of the stye?" I wanted to know.

"Get a baked potato, wrap it up nice and hot, and put it on your eye," Dr. Weinberg said.

"Will that help?" I asked.

"No," he replied. "But at least you'll have something to eat."

The good doctor, who believes that laughter is the best medicine, then gave me an eye exam. I passed with limping colors.

"You have 20/30 vision in your left eye and 20/40 in your right," he said. "Not bad for someone of your age. And definitely not as bad as this one patient who put a paddle over one eye, covered his other eye with his hand, and said, 'I can't see.' And he didn't even have a stye."

"What about mine?" I asked.

"Put a warm compress on it," Dr. Weinberg said. "And enjoy the baked potato."

"The Winner by a Nose"

Of all the famous bridges in America — the Brooklyn, the Golden Gate, and, of course, Beau and Jeff Bridges — the most impressive is the Zezima Bridge, which spans a great natural landmark: my nose.

So prominent is my proboscis that I could have set up a toll on the bridge — using SneezyPass — and made money to pay for a procedure that was performed not by a road crew but by Dr. Gregory Diehl, a sensational plastic surgeon with a practice in Port Jefferson Station, New York.

I first saw Dr. Diehl a few years ago, shortly after my dermatologist told me that I had a basal cell carcinoma, a common type of skin cancer that another doctor removed via Mohs surgery, which did not, fortunately, involve Larry and Curly.

The next day, Dr. Diehl expertly took skin from the upper right side of my nose and used it to seamlessly cover the area that was removed during the operation.

As sometimes happens, however, scar tissue developed. So I went back for a revision.

"I am going to do a dermabrasion," Dr. Diehl said, referring to a procedure to smooth out surface scarring.

"What will you be using?" I asked.

"A sander," he replied.

"Did you get it at Home Depot?" I wondered.

"That's where I get all my tools," Dr. Diehl said with a smile.

"This one must be big if you're going to sand my nose," I remarked.

"It's small, like a Dremel," said Dr. Diehl, referring to a make of rotary-action power tools.

"I've never heard of it," I confessed.

"I guess you don't know your way around a garage or a workshop," said Dr. Diehl. "I'm pretty handy. I work with wood to put up shelves and make flower boxes."

"This is why I'm not a carpenter," I said.

"Or a plastic surgeon," said Dr. Diehl, adding that he also would make a small incision on the right side of my nose to remove scar tissue that had built up under the skin. "And I won't even need a power tool."

On the day of the procedure, Dr. Diehl took a felt-tipped pen and drew lines on the areas of my nose where he would be working.

"You have a flair for this," I told him as I looked in a mirror to admire his artwork.

In the operating room in the back of his office, Dr. Diehl — ably assisted by certified surgical technologist Ann Rich — numbed my nose (not with an elephant dart) and began to work miracles.

In less than an hour, the surgery was over.

"You did great," Dr. Diehl said.

"It was nothing," I replied.

Ann said to put Bacitracin on the affected areas and told me how to change the dressing, which I had to do daily.

A week later, I returned so she could remove the sutures.

When Dr. Diehl came in, he examined my nose, grinned broadly, and exclaimed, "I nailed it!"

"I know you're handy," I said, "but if you actually did nail it, you would have broken the hammer."

"I've seen a lot of noses," said Dr. Diehl, who's sixty-one and has been in practice for twenty-nine years. "You have a nice one. It's very symmetrical. And now it looks even better."

He added that he has seen countless cases of basal cell carcinoma and that his greatest pleasure is "getting somebody out of a tight spot."

"Do you have any celebrity patients?" I asked.

"You're the most famous one," he said.

"You may not be the plastic surgeon to the stars," I said, "but you're a star in my book."

"That's why we call Dr. Diehl the real deal," said Ann.

"Take care of that beautiful nose," the good doctor said as I was leaving. "And stay away from power tools."

"Let's Get Physical"

As a geezer whose idea of physical fitness is doing twelve-ounce curls and getting up twice a night to go to the bathroom, I had always thought that exercise and health food will kill you.

Then I decided, after packing pathetically paunchy pandemic poundage, to join a gym.

Even though I have maintained my boyish figure and weigh in at a trim one hundred and eighty pounds, which is distributed nicely over my six-foot frame, looks can be deceiving. So I figured that my sedentary lifestyle needed adjustment, if only to have an excuse to stop eating the many vegetables that Sue, a longtime gym member, often makes as part of what she calls a "balanced diet."

Since I think a "balanced diet" is either spaghetti and meatballs or hot dogs and beans, I relented and signed up at Planet Fitness for a day pass, which I hoped wouldn't lead to a bypass.

Sue and I showed up after dinner (chicken and, of course, vegetables) and saw that the gym was, according to Sue, uncharacteristically crowded.

"Maybe all these people are here to see if I'll need CPR," I theorized.

That was a distinct possibility after a grueling half-hour workout, which was broken down into ten minutes each on a stationary bike, a treadmill, and an elliptical machine.

"I'm not going anywhere," I said as I pedaled furiously, two bikes over from Sue because the gym practices safe social distancing.

Since I was wearing a mask, which made it hard to gasp for air, she mercifully didn't hear me.

At the end of ten minutes, I had logged 1.61 miles and burned forty-seven calories.

I did even worse on the treadmill, going 0.34 miles and burning thirty-four calories.

The final indignity came on the elliptical machine, where I went 0.57 miles and burned fifty-five calories.

"Are you done?" asked Sue, looking fresh as a daisy.

"Huff, huff, huff!" I responded.

When we got home, I gulped down a beer.

"You're having beer after working out?" Sue said incredulously.

"Why not?" I replied. "It's better than broccoli."

In fact, I felt so invigorated that I signed up for a gym membership.

Two days later, I met Joe Robles, a personal trainer who asked what I wanted to accomplish.

"My main goal," I said, "is to stay alive."

"I think we can help," said Joe, who is thirty-one.

When I told him that I'm sixty-seven, he said, "Get out!"

"My membership sure didn't last long," I said.

"No, I mean you look a lot younger," Joe said. "And you're in pretty good shape."

"I owe it all to beer," I said, adding that I had a cold one after working out with Sue.

"One is OK," Joe said. "It's empty calories."

"My head is empty," I remarked, "so maybe that's where the calories go."

Then I told Joe about my pathetic performance a couple of nights before.

"I was slower than a tortoise with a broken leg," I said.

"You have to pace yourself and come up with a workout plan," said Joe, who suggested that I go to the gym three times a week and do short exercises, including weightlifting on the Smith machine.

"If I don't keel over," I asked, "would you rename it the Zezima machine?"

"That would be awesome!" Joe said.

"Until today, my personal trainers have been my wife and my grandchildren," I said. "They've kept me in good shape. Now it's up to you."

"I know I can handle it," said Joe. "We have everything you need here."

"Does that include beer?" I asked.

"Unfortunately, we don't have any," Joe said. "But that doesn't mean you can't have one when you get home. It'll hit the spot after you work out."

"I'll tell my wife what you said," I replied happily. "She'll be amazed to know that my exercise regimen still includes twelve-ounce curls."

CHAPTER 8

(When you reach a certain age, relaxing becomes an art form, whether it's in a lounge chair watching game shows or in a hammock drinking beer. Just make sure the hammock isn't eaten by mice.)

"Big Wheel Keep on Playing"

I am a man of many words. Unfortunately, most of them are incomprehensible when I use them in a sentence. And the rest can't be repeated in polite company.

This may explain why, even though I'm a writer who is spectacularly unqualified to do anything else, I am lousy at word games. I can't say the same for Sue, a retired teacher's assistant, or Guillaume, a scientist whose first language isn't even English.

Still, that has not stopped me from applying to be a contestant on the ultimate word game: "Wheel of Fortune."

Whenever I watch the program, with Pat Sajak hosting and Vanna White turning the letters, I solve my fair share of puzzles, unless they're in a category like "What are you doing?" ("I'm watching the show — what do you think I'm doing?" is never the right answer) or its equally difficult twin, "What are you wearing?" ("Nothing" is always wrong, too, and can lead to legal trouble.)

But when I watch "Wheel of Fortune" with Sue and Guillaume, the only thing I know for sure is that I would never win a fortune if I were spinning the wheel for real with them.

That's why I hope they don't apply to be contestants, too. In fact, they are so good at word games that they have routinely beaten me in "Scrabble," which I also lost to Katie and Lauren when they were in grade school and to Sue's late grandmother, who at the time was still alive, giving her an unfair advantage.

Where I really get walloped is in "7 Little Words," which is in the daily newspaper.

Here are the instructions: "Find the 7 words to match the 7 clues. The numbers in parentheses represent the number of letters in each solution. Each letter combination can be used only once, but all letter combinations will be necessary to complete the puzzle."

One clue was: "Annual delphinium relative." It had eight letters.

Answer (which I never would have gotten): "Larkspur."

"I like playing this game because it keeps my mind sharp," Sue has told me, being too kind to say that it would do me some good as well.

If she's stumped, she'll ask Alexa.

"That's cheating," I have said on more than one occasion.

"You cheat at Scrabble," Sue has responded, again being too kind to say that it doesn't do me any good. I'm grateful that she also doesn't mention her grandmother.

If Guillaume — who was born in France and can make puns in two languages, a talent I greatly admire — is around, Sue will ask him for help. If he's not and Alex is stumped, too, Sue will call him with a particularly vexing clue, which Guillaume always gets.

It goes without saying, but I'll say it anyway, that my beloved wife is seldom desperate enough to ask me for help. And if she is, I always have — you guessed it — no clue.

Nonetheless, I am confident in my chances of getting on "Wheel of Fortune." To apply, I went to the website and filled out a form with basic information like name (I looked it up on my driver's license) and address (ditto). Then I uploaded a photo of myself (I hope it doesn't scare Vanna).

I also recorded a brief video saying why I should be a contestant.

"Here's your chance to charm us!" it said in the instructions. "Try to follow these tips when creating your video."

Some of the tips were:

Don't look like you just rolled out of bed.

Smile.

Be natural.

Don't ramble.

HAVE FUN!

If I get on the show, I'll bring Sue and Guillaume for moral support. I'll even bring some loose change in case I want to buy a vowel. I just hope Pat doesn't ask me what I'm wearing.

"When the Cat's Away, the Hammock Won't Sway"

Before I retired, I was often accused of lying down on the job. Now that I'm not working, it's my job to lie down.

And what better place to do it than in my brand-new hammock.

I needed a new hammock because my old one, which I've had for at least a dozen years, was eaten by mice.

I had always thought that mice ate cheese, though where they get the money to buy it, or if they have it with wine and crackers, is a mystery.

But one or more of the rascally rodents chewed through the ropes of my hammock, which I have kept in the shed so it would be protected, not only from the elements, but from hungry critters like — you guessed it — moose.

No, I mean mice.

The first inkling I had that my hammock wasn't in the best of shape, just like the guy who owns it, was when I took it out, attached the rings on the ends to the corresponding hooks on two posts, plopped myself in, promptly fell through, and hit the ground with a thud on my backside, although I did not, thank goodness, spill my beer.

Bottoms up!

I disentangled myself and noticed that several of the braided ropes had come loose. I tried to tie them together but to no avail.

Sue, who bought me the hammock, saw tufts of rope on the ground and, later, in the shed.

"I hate to say this," she said, and proceeded to say it anyway, "but I think this is the work of a mouse."

"Mice don't eat rope," I responded, with absolutely no authority, "unless they want to get some fiber in their diet."

Still, Sue suggested that I stand on a lawn chair, one of the few things in the shed that are of any practical use, including me, and check out the loft where I keep the hammock.

Sure enough, I saw little brown droppings.

"It's a mouse all right," I told Sue. "Or maybe a family of them: mommy, daddy, and baby."

The Three Stooges' theme song, "Three Blind Mice," began running through the cavern that is my skull. In one classic Stooge short, the boys were exterminators who brought their own mice to the house where they'd been hired to get rid of them.

"This never would have happened if Henry were still alive," I told Sue, recalling one of our four cats. Henry routinely assassinated little creatures — birds, bunnies, and, of course, mice — and brought them to us as gifts.

Sadly, like the other family felines, Henry went to that big litter box in the sky. Now the field mice are having a field day. And they're eating my hammock. So Sue bought me a new one.

There's just one problem: It's too long. The first time I set it up and plopped myself in, I hit the ground with a thud, though this time I didn't fall through.

The new hammock is a foot longer than the old one, meaning I can't lie in it with a beer and swing myself to either sleep or stupor.

I emailed the hammock company and got a quick response from someone named Nova, who said they don't make a shorter hammock and suggested I try to shorten the new one myself.

I wouldn't know how, so I went to a home improvement store to buy new hooks, which I planned to insert higher up on the two posts. But a friendly employee named John looked at the photos I took of the posts, which are old, cracked, and splintered (a good name for a law firm), and said the new hooks probably wouldn't hold.

Now I'm hoping to get new posts or find someone with a post hole digger to move the present ones farther apart.

In the meantime, I think I'll buy a mousetrap. It'll be cheaper than getting another cat.

"May the Pest Man Win"

My house is bugged. Not with listening devices because the listeners (the CIA, the FBI, Russia) would soon be fast asleep after discovering that I lead a singularly dull life.

No, I mean with real bugs.

This really bugs Sue, who hates the little critters so much that she prowls the house with a flyswatter, ready to annihilate the latest winged or crawly invader and add it to her daily scoresheet. She is an otherwise gentle person who would, indeed, hurt a fly.

One day, Sue killed nine of them.

"That's enough for a baseball team," I said. "I guess they don't know about the infield fly rule."

Sue ignored the remark and asked, "Where do they come from?"

"Mommy flies," I answered. "We should put up a sign saying, 'No fly zone.' That would keep them out."

Sue ignored that remark, too, and used a shoe to smash a spider that was roughly the size of a Chihuahua.

"I'm going to call an exterminator," she said.

"For me?" I stammered.

"I'll have to see how much they charge," said Sue.

A couple of days and a dozen dead insects later, we were visited by Jack the Pest Control Guy.

"My wife says I'm a pest," I told Jack. "You're not going to exterminate me, are you?"

"No," Jack said reassuringly. "I don't have enough bug spray for that."

"What's the critter that people complain about the most?" I asked.

"Ants," Jack answered. "I find them in basements and bathrooms, on chairs and tables, and in kitchens for sure."

"Has anyone ever told you that they had ants in their pants?" I wanted to know.

"Actually, yes," said Jack.

"It must have been a brief encounter," I said before telling Jack about one of my favorite 1950s sci-fi movies, "Them!"

"It's about ants that grow to a gigantic size after being exposed to nuclear radiation," I explained. "They end up in the sewers of Los Angeles and have to be killed with flamethrowers."

"I guess my bug spray wouldn't work on them, either," Jack said.

"If I used a flamethrower to kill the ants in our kitchen, I'd burn the house down," I said.

"Then your wife would call me back here to get rid of you," Jack predicted.

"How about spiders?" I inquired.

"We get lots of calls about them," said Jack. "But they're actually good because they kill other bugs."

"They might be costing you business," I said before telling Jack about another classic science fiction flick, "The Incredible Shrinking Man," the story of a man who is exposed to a mysterious mist and begins to melt away.

"At the end, he's so small that he's attacked by a spider," I said. "He kills it with a pin that looks like a spear compared to him."

"I'd need a lot of pins to kill all the spiders I've dealt with," said Jack, adding that he has never seen "The Incredible Shrinking Man" but did enjoy "Honey, I Shrunk the Kids."

"Are you married?" I asked.

"No," Jack said, "but I have a girlfriend."

"Does she hate bugs as much as my wife does?" I said.

"Yes," said Jack. "She'll call me to say there's a fly behind the refrigerator."

"Does she expect you to leave work and go home to get rid of it?" I asked.

"Yes," Jack said. "She's scared of spiders and ants and things like that."

"You could be her hero," I said.

Jack smiled, looked down at his shirt with the pest control company's logo on the front, and said, "She likes a man in uniform."

"My wife and I are a swat team," I said. "I find the bugs in the house and she swats them."

"You should have a lot less of them now," Jack said when he was finished.

"Thanks," Sue said. Then she pointed to me and added, "If I find any other pests in the house, I'll give you a call."

"My Chair, Lady"

As a guy who takes most things sitting down, I couldn't stand the thought that my favorite chair had hit bottom.

But that's what happened when the seat of power was pulled out from under me for a major reupholstering job.

My throne (the only one in the house not situated in the bathroom) had seen better days. And nights, because that was when I used it the most, mainly to watch movies or sporting events, the endings of which I seldom saw because I had dozed off while holding popcorn or beer that slipped from my grasp and — you guessed it — spilled all over the chair.

But that's not the main reason why this mangy piece of furniture, which is twenty-five years old (one hundred and seventy-five in human years), needed repair.

The primary cause of its pathetic condition was feline frolic.

We used to have cats. Before they went to that big litter box in the sky, the destructive demons used the chair as their own personal scratching post. The poor thing looked like it had been attacked by a mountain lion in heat.

Sue covered the chair with a chair cover (sorry if I am getting too technical) and made me move it to the living room, where I was banished when I didn't want to watch one of the approximately seven hundred home improvement shows that Sue loves to watch while seated comfortably in her newer, much nicer chair in the family room.

In fact, Sue's chair used to be mine. It's the latest in a series of seats that were originally mine but fell into the hands (or paws) of various humans (or animals), including my wife, our daughters, our grandchildren, the aforementioned cats, and even a dog that would plop herself down in my former chair and either watch Animal Planet or fall asleep while snoring and drooling, probably because she had seen me do the same thing.

Finally, Sue decided that my present chair — which used to be mine, was taken over by her, then went to the dog, and, since the purchase of two better chairs, is now mine again — needed an upgrade.

So she called Loli's and Carlos' Upholstery. The day after Sue and I visited the store to pick out new upholstery (Sue picked it out while I stood there like a bobblehead doll, silently nodding and smiling at her choice), Loli's and Carlos's son, Danny, and son-in-law, Juan, came over to pick up the chair.

"It's old," Danny said after Sue had taken off the cover to reveal leg wounds, arm scars, and cushion lumps.

"I'm old, too," I remarked. "Will I get reupholstered?"

"No, you're in pretty good shape," said Danny, adding that guys often lose their chairs to their wives and kids. "And," he noted, sizing me up as a geezer, "their grandkids."

"Have you guys ever lost your chairs?" I asked.

"Yes," Danny answered.

"Yes," repeated Juan.

Then the terrific twosome carried my chair out the front door, lifted it into the company truck, and drove away.

A week or so later, they were back with a chair I didn't recognize.

"Wow!" Sue exclaimed.

"Is this the same one?" I wondered.

"Yes," Juan said.

"My father reupholstered it," Danny told us.

"Does he have a chair?" I asked.

"He has a recliner," Danny replied. "He reupholstered it, too."

"Has your mother taken it?" I wanted to know.

"No," Danny said. "He won't let her."

I looked at Sue, who didn't look back. But she did sit in the repaired chair, which sported beige upholstery with a diamond pattern.

"Now it's comfortable," Sue declared. "No more sagging in the middle of the cushion."

When Sue got up, I sat down.

"This is great!" I said. "I may sit here all day."

I stayed in the chair after Danny and Juan left.

"Is there a game tonight or a movie?" Sue asked. "Are you going to have popcorn? Be careful! Don't drop kernels so they get wedged under the cushion."

"Do I have to wear clean pants?" I inquired.

"Yes," said Sue. "And no greasy hands!"

"OK," I said. "Just don't take my chair. It's the one thing I won't stand for."

"The Bricklayer's Apprentice"

A man's home is his hassle. That's especially true if he's me, the Least Handy Man in America, a guy who thinks a screwdriver is vodka and orange juice.

But being dumb as a brick didn't stop me from using bricks to help lay the foundation for a job that shored up the foundation.

It was all part of a home improvement project in which the house got new vinyl siding, not just on the side, but in the front and the back, for what Sue and I hope will be the vinyl time.

The work was done by a terrific contractor named Anthony Amini, who owns Performance Contracting and Management, the company that Sue and I previously used for putting on a new roof, installing a new floor, and, yes, changing light bulbs, a task so simple that it is beyond my comprehension.

How many columnists does it take to change a light bulb? One — if he hires someone else to do it.

Anyway, Anthony and his hardworking crew replaced the faded old siding with beautiful, Nantucket gray strips, which give our Colonial a look so fresh that a real estate agent, who's selling the vastly inferior ranch across the street, raved about it.

It's so good that drivers even slow down at the stop sign in front of our house (instead of blowing through, as they usually do) to admire Anthony's handiwork, which includes new gutters, window moldings, and all kinds of other things I'm not familiar with because I am, after all, dumb as a brick.

But I got somewhat smarter when I helped Andy Campanile, a bricklayer par excellence, fix a broken corner of the foundation.

"It looks like your joint failed," Andy told me.

"I'm old," I replied. "All my joints are failing."

"No, I mean this," he said, pointing to a separated block the approximate size and consistency of my skull.

"Does that make me a blockhead?" I wondered.

"If you say so," said Andy, who also does masonry, plumbing, and tiling.

"How about electrical work?" I asked.

"My uncle and cousins do that. I do pretty much everything else," said Andy, who's fifty-four and got started at age twelve with his late father, Andrew Sr. "I carried his homemade toolbox when I was a kid. It was so heavy! I learned a lot from the old guys. Now I'm the old guy."

"You're a youngster," I said, adding that I'm sixty-seven. "My father was the handiest guy I ever knew. Unfortunately, it skipped a generation."

That didn't stop Andy from accepting my generous offer (it was free) to help him repair a corner of the foundation.

"We're going to use mortar mix," Andy said.

"The mortar the merrier!" I chirped.

The remark amused Anthony's sixteen-year-old son, Mateo, a wonderful young man who is learning handiness from his father the way Andy learned it from his.

My father, who was my hero, tried to teach me handiness but soon realized I was ambidextrous — incompetent with both hands.

Undeterred, Andy showed me how to pour the mortar into a pan, add water, and mix it with a mason's trowel. Mateo, who also asked to help, displayed a natural talent that made me want to throw in the trowel.

"What if you get the mortar on you?" Mateo asked.

"You become part of the foundation," I said.

Then Andy showed us how to use the trowel to put wet mortar on a brick, one of many that would be used in place of the failed joint.

Andy did most of the rebuilding himself, after which he stuccoed the corner using another trowel, this one with a sponge finish.

"May I try?" I asked.

"Sure," said Andy, who handed me the trowel and told me that his last name means "bell tower" in Italian. "When I was in Venice," he recalled as I worked away, "I went into this bar called Bar Al Campanile. I said, 'I have to be related somehow. Where's my free drink?' They wouldn't give me one."

I thought Andy would need a drink after seeing my handiwork, but he and Anthony thought I did a good job.

"Perfect!" Anthony declared.

"You must be Italian!" Andy chimed in.

"Actually, I am," I said. "And for the first time in my life, I don't feel dumb as a brick."

"Wheel of Misfortune"

I know I'm not letter perfect — my last name begins with the last letter of the alphabet, which is good only for catching some Z's — but I never realized just how imperfect I am until I flunked an audition for "Wheel of Fortune."

I applied to be on the show by going on the "Wheel" website and filling out a questionnaire with basic information, starting with my name, which I spelled correctly.

Then I recorded a video on which I said I am a longtime "Wheel of Fortune" fan who could bring a lot of good-natured humor to the program.

"Who knows, I might even win," I added. "And I'll bring some loose change so I can buy vowels."

About a week later, I got an email inviting me to try out. If I did well, I could get on the show, where I'd meet host Pat Sajak and letter turner Vanna White. And if I had good luck spinning the wheel and I solved enough puzzles, I might win a fortune.

Little did I know that I would hit "BANKRUPT" before I even started.

My audition, which was conducted on Zoom, was hosted by Jackie Lamatis, the show's personable contestant coordinator.

Also trying out were Meaghan Polensky and Bianca Addison, who were very nice, very young, and, unfortunately for me, very smart.

In the first round, Meaghan and Bianca solved all the puzzles. I did buzz in first on one of them and shouted, "Volleyball tournament." But

I didn't realize until a nanosecond too late that the last word was plural, which prompted Bianca to buzz in and say, "Volleyball tournaments."

"Was the S really the dollar sign I didn't get?" I asked.

"I think so," said Jackie, who asked us to introduce ourselves.

Meaghan said she is a fourth-grade teacher and Bianca said she wants to get into the entertainment field.

When it was my turn, I noted that both women are in their twenties, making them four decades younger than I am. To compound matters, I added, I am on the same intellectual level as Meaghan's students. I also said I am a nationally syndicated newspaper columnist whose work has no redeeming social value. And I'm the author of several books, all of which are crimes against literature.

"You're really funny," Jackie told me.

"If you insist," I replied. "At this rate, it's probably the only thing that would qualify me to be on the show."

Sadly, I proved it in the subsequent rounds. A few days earlier, when I practiced online, I solved every puzzle. Of course, I wasn't competing against anyone. In the audition, two things stood in my way of victory: Meaghan and Bianca.

Round 2 was a blur. The only thing I remember was the jingle that played while I tried futilely to guess the answers. It sounded like this: Dumb-dumb-de-dumb-dumb DUMB DUMB!

In the last round, each contestant played alone while the other two waited, unable to see or hear what was going on.

Naturally, I went last. Jackie showed me four groups of four puzzles, each of which was partially filled with letters. The first three categories were "Thing," "Before and After," and "Place."

I didn't solve even one puzzle.

The last category was "TV Show Titles." Miraculously, I got three of the four.

"How come you didn't have 'Wheel of Fortune' as one of the titles?" I asked.

"We get asked that question a lot," Jackie replied.

But my rally clearly wasn't enough to make up for my overall performance, which was — to use a word that would have been perfect in the "Thing" category — pathetic.

At the end of the hourlong audition, Jackie got me, Meaghan, and Bianca back on and thanked us for participating.

"Wait a month," Jackie said. "If you haven't heard back from us, you probably weren't chosen to be on the show."

"Would I get some lovely parting gifts?" I wondered.

"Back in the day you would," Jackie stated.

"I guess this isn't the day," I said.

"No," said Jackie. "But you've been a lot of fun."

"Give my best to Pat and Vanna," I said, knowing I wouldn't be called back. "And now that I don't have to buy vowels, I can keep my loose change."

CHAPTER 9

(Buying the farm is never a pleasant thought for oldsters. But visiting one is a different story. So is apple picking, helping the grandkids with a lemonade stand, and other fun stuff.)

"Farmer Pepper's Lonely Heartburn Band"

I like to think I'm hot stuff, even in winter, but whenever I look in the mirror to shave, I come to the sad realization that I'm not so sizzling after all.

Still, I almost needed to call the fire department when I ate some peppers I picked at a farm whose owner is one cool dude.

"What does it take to be a farmer?" I asked Doug Cooper, who owns Cooper Farms in Mattituck, New York.

"A strong back and a weak mind," he replied.

"I have both," I assured him.

"You're just the man for the job," he said.

Mr. Cooper, as he is known in these parts, resembles the late actor Gary Cooper, who was tall, dark, and handsome, and has the same laconic way of speaking.

When I said I like his corn, he said, "Shucks."

I wasn't surprised because his farm stand features these signs:

" 'Lettuce' supply your farm fresh needs!"

"Our beets are 'unbeetable!'"

"Ask about our 'eggcellent' eggs!"

"What about your eggs?" I asked.

"We let our chickens take care of them," said Mr. Cooper, who not only has a flourishing flock of fowl, but also a pair of peacock parents and, he added, "two baby ones."

"This place is for the birds," I said.

At that precise moment, a rooster crowed, "Cock-a-doodle-doo!"

It's been a wake-up call at the family-owned farm for two hundred years.

"I'm not that old," said Mr. Cooper, who is seventy-three. "I was born on April 2, 1948. My mother said, 'I'm having twins.' My father said, 'April Fools' Day was yesterday.' It was no joke. My brother, Donald, is ten minutes younger than me."

I put my arm around Sue and said, "April 2 is our anniversary. No fooling."

Mr. Cooper then regaled us with the story of "The Squirrel That Got Away."

Years ago, the rascally rodent came in the house through a window screen and was trapped in a box by Mr. Cooper's late father, David, who took the box outside and blasted it with a shotgun. The squirrel survived and ran away, only to come back through the window screen and was trapped again, this time in a burlap bag, which the elder Cooper took outside and blasted with a shotgun. The squirrel escaped through a hole in the bag and came back a third time.

"That was the charm," said Mr. Cooper. "It wasn't the smartest squirrel, but it was lucky, so we took it down to the field and set it free."

It was that very field to which Sue and I towed a wagon that Mr. Cooper gave us to pick vegetables, including hot peppers, which Sue loves and I don't.

"They'll blow your brains out," she said.

"Not mine," I responded. "I don't have any."

Sue nodded as we made our way through rows of peppers — cherry, chili, corkscrew, habanero, and jalapeño — that I dutifully picked and plopped into a cardboard box in the wagon.

Mr. Cooper had left by the time we got back to the stand with our bounty, which included corn, beets, and tomatoes. We paid a grand total of $17.25 and drove home with a vehicle of veggies.

A few nights later, Sue made pork chops with onions and the cherry peppers I had picked.

I took one bite. A smoke alarm went off in my mouth.

"Ung, ung, ung!" I cried as I fanned my tongue with a napkin.

"Is your nose running?" Sue asked.

"It's lumbering," I said, choking out a response.

I tried to douse the invisible flames with water. It didn't work.

"Have some bread," Sue said.

It helped. So did red wine, which probably prevented me from having a heart attack.

Sue smiled as she calmly ate the chops and peppers, which had no effect on her.

I tried to be brave by having a few more forkfuls, but each time, I repeated the routine: gag, gulp, gong.

"Dinner's delicious," I told Sue, "but if I eat any more, I'm going to buy the farm."

"Tell that to Mr. Cooper," she said.

"He already knows I have a weak mind," I said. "Now I can tell him I'm hot stuff, too."

"It All Comes Out in the Wash"

This may sound like a shameful admission — and it would be if I had any shame — but my body hadn't been cleaned, my top scrubbed, and my rear end buffed in more than a year.

So I went to the car wash.

It was the first time since I got my SUV (sloppy utility vehicle) that I had brought it in for a bath. And there was a lot to bathe away: bird droppings, tree gunk, flower pollen, road salt, street dirt, and all kinds of other stuff that made my car a partner in grime.

I drove to Island Car Wash and encountered the automotive equivalent of a Cecil B. DeMille epic. When I finally reached the booth, a friendly attendant named Jason asked which treatment I wanted.

I looked over the sign with all the choices and said, "Give me the works."

"That would be the Platinum package," Jason told me. "What scent would you like?"

"How about beer?" I replied.

"We don't have that one," said Jason, adding that the fragrances included strawberry and black ice. "They're my favorites," he said. "We also have new-car scent."

"My car isn't new, but this is its first wash, so I'll take it," I said, handing Jason my debit card so he could charge me forty-seven dollars.

"Don't forget to roll up your windows," he reminded me after giving the card back.

"Thanks," I said. "I didn't bring my bathing suit."

Going through the car wash was like being on an amusement park ride in Niagara Falls.

Slowly I rolled, step by step, inch by inch, until my vehicle came out the other side. I turned left into an empty space, exited the car, and watched as a quartet of cleaners armed with rags, spray bottles, and vacuum cleaner hoses descended on the dark green auto, making it pristine inside and out.

"They're doing a great job," I told supervisor Celso Bocchini.

"My four best people are working on your car," said Celso, who told me that the Premium package included "vacuuming, car wash, windows in and out, waxing, rims, shiny stuff on the tires, and scent."

"My car was filthy, but it's looking good now," I said. "At least the inside wasn't too bad."

"You'd be surprised at what we find in some cars," said Celso. "You don't know what will be in there. We find a lot of popcorn and french fries. We once found a couple of hot dogs that were almost walking. I don't know how people can drive around with that kind of stuff in their cars."

"Can I help clean my car?" I asked.

"You can do anything you want," Celso answered. "It's your car."

He handed me a damp cloth.

"A dry one will scratch your car," he said. "Now put some elbow grease into it."

The grease had already been washed off, but my elbow was sore after buffing the hood and the front passenger-side door.

"Did I do a good job?" I wondered.

"Yes," said Celso. "Make believe you do something and take credit."

"Is your car nice and clean?" I asked.

"It's a mess," Celso confessed. "It gets washed when I have a chance, but it's less than anybody else here. That should tell you something."

"It tells me that you're a busy guy," I said.

Celso nodded and pointed to his car, a 2001 Hyundai Sonata that was parked across the lot.

"It has only eighty thousand miles on it," he said. "I bought it for two thousand dollars five years ago. I've put only thirty thousand miles on it in five years. I drive five miles a day. I don't need a BMW, but if you want to give me one, I'll take it."

"I'll have to get a job so I can afford it," I said before getting in my shiny, spanking clean, beautifully scented vehicle.

"You can work here," Celso said. "Maybe then I can get my car washed."

"The Story of Jerry Applehead"

According to the history books, which I used to read only before final exams, there once was an American pioneer named Johnny Appleseed, who introduced apple trees to large parts of the Midwest, where they produced fruit that personal computers were eventually named after.

An updated part of the story concerns Johnny's disreputable cousin, Jerry Applehead, who took his wife, Sue, apple picking and littered the orchard with his stupid jokes.

Our adventure began when Sue and I drove to Lewin Farms and met Gabrielle, a very nice young woman who worked at the orchard stand.

"Would you like a basket?" she asked.

"I'm a basket case, so why not?" I answered.

"That will be five dollars," Gabrielle said.

"Do you have change of a hundred?" I inquired.

"Yes, I do," said Gabrielle.

"Unfortunately, I don't have a hundred, so here's a five," I said, handing her the fin and taking the basket.

Then Sue and I headed out into the orchard.

The apples were, if I do say so (and I'm about to), ripe for picking. And there were plenty to choose from, mostly Mac, Gala, and Honeycrisp, though the orchard also has Delicious (both Red and Golden), Royal Court, Cortland, Cameo, Rome, Fuji, Granny Smith, and Stayman.

When Katie and Lauren were kids, we took them apple picking every year. We've also taken Chloe and Lilly. But this year, Sue and I went solo and pretty much had the place to ourselves, thanks to Sue's brilliant idea to go during the week so we could avoid traffic that would have rivaled rush hour in New York City, otherwise known as, yes, the Big Apple.

"There are a lot of big apples here," I said as I plucked several Macs and dropped them into the basket.

Sue, meanwhile, picked some of her favorite apples: Golden Delicious.

"You're going for the gold," I told her. "And I bet they're delicious."

I'm surprised she didn't bop me on the head with one. At least it would have made apple sauce.

I rattled off all kinds of other apple products: apple pie, apple cobbler, apple juice, apple cider, apple butter, apple fritters, apple strudel, baked apples, and candy apples.

"How do you like them apples?" I asked.

Sue looked like she needed a bottle of applejack.

When the basket was full, I lugged it back to the stand, where Gabrielle put it on a scale.

"The apples are twenty-three and a half pounds," she said. "So it comes to fifty dollars."

I searched my wallet, but I had only forty dollars. Sue had no money.

"We only take cash," Gabrielle said.

Another customer offered to give me ten bucks, but I politely declined.

"There's an ATM in the farm store," said Gabrielle, adding that she would hold our apples until we returned.

Sue and I drove about a mile down the road, withdrew some money, and drove back to the orchard, where I gave Gabrielle fifty dollars.

"Does ATM stand for apple teller machine?" I wondered.

"It should," said Gabrielle. "We had a customer recently who said we should accept Apple Pay. And there was another customer who spent a hundred and ninety-eight dollars on apples. He came with a dolly."

"I guess he had his own apple support," I remarked.

"Just ignore him," Sue told Gabrielle.

"Why?" I said. "Because I'm rotten to the core?"

Then I asked Gabrielle what her favorite kind of apple is.

"Honeycrisp," said Gabrielle, a recent college graduate. "They're pretty much everyone's favorite."

"And they're bright red, just like your fingernails," I noted.

"My nails were supposed to be pink," Gabrielle said. "But I guess red is more appropriate here."

"I'm lucky I didn't break a nail when I picked all these apples," I said.

"When we get home," Sue announced, "I'm going to make an apple crisp."

"That sounds delicious," said Gabrielle.

"Delicious?" I said, pointing out her inadvertent pun. "You're catching on!"

Gabrielle smiled and said, "Thank you, guys, for brightening my day."

"This adventure will go down in the history books," I told Sue as we headed back to the car.

"Except for your stupid jokes," she replied.

"In the immortal words of Donny Osmond," I said, "one bad apple don't spoil the whole bunch, girl."

"Weather Stick Rains Supreme"

Maybe it's because my head is in the clouds, or the heat is really getting to me, but I like to think I can predict the weather better than the National Weather Service.

And unlike such respected TV weather anchors as Lonnie Quinn and Al Roker, I don't use radar, satellites, or European models. In fact, I have always thought the best European model is Heidi Klum.

At any rate, I owe my prodigious prognosticating powers to the greatest meteorological device ever devised.

I refer, of course, to the Davis Hill Weather Stick.

It is, yes, a stick that rises or falls depending on, yes, the weather. If it's sunny and dry, which is perfect for lying in a hammock with a beer, the thin piece of wood points upward. But if it's cloudy and humid, often a harbinger of rain, which means I have to go inside for a brew, the stick points downward.

What could be simpler? Or, at $6 a pop, cheaper?

To find out more about the amazing properties of the weather stick, several of which are now on my property, I called the Davis Hill Company in East Hardwick, Vermont, and spoke with "chief cook and bottle washer" Tim Hartt.

"I've been doing this for thirty-six years now and I sell twenty-five thousand of these things a year," said Tim, who's also a pig farmer. "The sticks keep me honest and put gas in the truck."

Because he grosses about seventy thousand dollars a year, that's a lot of gas.

"There's no money in farming," said Tim, who has "a little twenty-two-acre place with four hundred free-range meat birds, three or four hogs, and a laying flock of a hundred birds that lay a couple of dozen eggs a day."

"So in order to make ends meet," I suggested, "you have to get on the stick."

"I'm glad you said it, not me," replied Tim, who told me that the weather sticks are made from balsam fir trees. "Every tree in nature reacts to moisture in the air," he said, "but balsam firs react more dramatically. Their branches go up and down depending on how much moisture there is. So friends and I go into the woods during harvest, strip wood off the trees, and make weather sticks."

"Do they really work?" I asked.

"You bet," Tim answered. "And I have lots of satisfied customers to prove it. One of them, Donna from Medford, Oregon, called me the other day to say she needs more sticks to give out. She bought a dozen in 2018 to give to special people in her life. My typical customer is a little old lady who will call me to say she needs another stick because her first one was eaten by a chipmunk."

"If meteorologists had weather sticks," I said, "their forecasts would be more accurate."

"As long as they can keep the chipmunks away," said Tim, sixty-three, a husband, father, and grandfather who said he just looks out the window to see what it's doing.

"Animals are pretty good at predicting the weather," I noted. "I had a dog that knew when it was going to rain. She'd hide under the table because she was afraid of thunder. She should have been a forecaster on TV."

"Chickens know, too," Tim said. "They can tell when it's time to go in. The laying ones are smart. The meat birds are definitely dumber."

Even though I have been called a birdbrain, I was smart enough to order a weather stick from Tim, who had to cut the conversation short because, he said, "the chickens are calling me."

A few days later, a bunch of sticks arrived in the mail. I nailed one to a door frame outside, under an eave, as recommended, and told Sue that it was going to rain.

"How do you know?" she asked.

"The weather stick is pointing downward," I told her.

Sure enough, it was soon raining cats, dogs, and chickens. When it cleared up and the sun came out, the stick pointed upward.

"Works like a charm," I said. "I should send one of these sticks to the National Weather Service."

"A Farewell to Fins"

It is with a heavy heart and stewed gills that I announce the passing of Camilla, our beloved and semi-intelligent betta fish, who tragically succumbed to water on the brain and now sleeps with all of our other fishes.

Camilla, who should have been called Camillo because the fish was gender-fluid and very coy, though not koi, died at the ripe old age of two.

She was the longest-living of the family's fabulous fleet of fine finny friends. The average lifespan of most of the other fish we have had over the years was approximately as long as the Super Bowl halftime show.

A notable exception was Curly, who survived for weeks after the demise of his bowl mates, Moe and Larry, who died within minutes of each other, probably in a suicide pact.

Curly was killed when I opened a kitchen cabinet and a bottle of vitamins fell out, conking him on the head.

Sue was aghast, as were the young Katie and Lauren, who wailed, "You killed our fish!"

I tried to soothe them with comforting words: "They were Mommy's vitamins."

Another standout was Pumpkin, out of whose bowl Ramona, the first and dumbest of our four cats (all of whom have since gone to that big litter box in the sky), liked to drink.

Pumpkin would play peekaboo with Ramona. The scaly scamp also liked to squirt the flummoxed feline, though Ramona never succeeded in gobbling up Mrs. Zezima's unfrozen fish stick.

I actually bonded with Pumpkin, who would greet me every day by swimming to the side of the bowl and gulping a silent "Good morning!" Then I would feed a flaky breakfast to the flaky fish.

When Pumpkin passed, at about a year old, Katie and Lauren sobbed uncontrollably during a solemn toilet-side service that concluded when their lifeless pal was flushed to kingdom come.

It was the same sad routine with all of our other, similarly doomed, shorter-lived goldfish, a couple of which didn't survive the car ride home from the pet store.

Then there was Camilla, whom we adopted a couple of years ago at the urging of Chloe and Lilly.

Sue and I drove with the girls to the pet store and bought a pink female betta fish and color-coordinated pink pebbles in the hope that we would be the cover story in Good Bowlkeeping.

Unfortunately, Camilla's bowl held only sixteen ounces of water, the same size as the bowl that houses Igor, a blue male betta fish that lives with Chloe and Lilly.

"You should get a larger bowl," a pet-store employee suggested.

I ignored the advice. Forty-eight hours later, Camilla went belly-up.

Unbeknownst to Chloe and Lilly — who also are unaware that the first two Igors had suffered the same fate and that the third one is now the charm — I launched Camilla into the porcelain version of Davy Jones's locker and bought another pink betta fish, this one a male that we also called Camilla.

The friendly fish, who had the same bubbly personality as the late, lamented Pumpkin, far exceeded its life expectancy, probably because I gave in and bought a one-gallon bowl that was a spacious mansion compared to the cramped condo where the original Camilla lived ever so briefly.

On visits to our house, Chloe and Lilly were none the wiser and always loved to feed Camilla the same drab food that nourished so many of our other fish.

I have not yet broken the news to the girls that their tiny friend has gone to fishy heaven, but Sue and I did have a respectful funeral that involved indoor plumbing.

Farewell, Camilla. Float in peace.

"Taking a Stand With Lemonade"

When life hands you lemons, goes an old saying, you will have a lot of car repair bills. That's why you should have a yard sale. And what better way to lure customers than with a lemonade stand.

That was the brilliant idea Chloe and Lilly had when Sue and Lauren decided to embark on this allegedly moneymaking enterprise.

The idea of the yard sale, which was held in Lauren's front yard, was to foist a bunch of junk that had been piling up in our respective houses on bargain-happy people who would, we hoped, pay fistfuls of cash for stuff they don't need, take it home, and make it their junk.

On the day of the big event, the lawn was filled with stuff, much of which was priceless, mainly because it wasn't worth anything.

In a prime spot was the lemonade stand.

Chloe wanted to charge three dollars a cup. Lauren said no, so Chloe suggested two dollars. Finally, it was decided that fifty cents was a fair price.

"OK," said Chloe. "But I want a tip jar."

That was nixed, too, though Chloe did prevail in charging twenty-five cents extra for Unicorn syrup, which is colored sugar water that could be added to the lemonade.

And there was enough to quench the thirst of the entire population of Luxembourg: two ninety-six-ounce bottles of "organic lemonade." We also had three small bottles of syrup (red, green, and purple), one hundred seven-ounce cups, and an equal number of ecologically correct straws.

The sale was supposed to begin at nine a.m. The first customer showed up at 8:15.

"How much is this stool?" she asked.

"Ordinarily, it's a thousand dollars," I replied, "but there's a special deal today for only five bucks."

"I'll take it," the woman said.

It was my only sale of the day.

Another woman came by and asked about a wine rack.

"I've lightened the load for you by drinking all the wine," I said.

She left without saying another word, probably because I had driven her to drink.

Someone else asked about a baby seat.

"It's three dollars," I said. "Baby not included."

Money wasn't included, either.

Chloe, eight, and Lilly, five, had better luck with other customers.

"We have lots of nice things!" Chloe chirped.

To which Lilly added, "Let's sell everything for free!"

"I can go for that," a man said.

Meanwhile, the lemonade stand was cleaning up. I poured the drinks, Lilly put in the syrup, and Chloe collected the money.

Unfortunately, the swarm of people was outnumbered by a swarm of bees.

"This must be a wasp neighborhood," I told a guy who didn't buy any lemonade but left a twenty-five-cent tip for the girls anyway.

When it was time for lunch, Chloe and I went inside for a peanut butter sandwich and a cup of lemonade each.

Then Lilly came in and had a bowl of macaroni and cheese. I had one, too.

"Have some lemonade," Lilly said.

I filled a cup, to which Lilly added red syrup.

Then she wanted me to have another cup with green syrup, followed by one with purple syrup. Lilly stirred all of them with paper straws.

"Why don't you have some?" I asked.

Lilly shook her head and said, "I don't like lemonade."

Seven cups later, I made a beeline — even though the bees were outside — to the porcelain convenience.

Back in the yard, a woman walked up with her young son and a pair of giant schnauzers, who smothered Chloe in kisses (the dogs, not the kid, who lapped up three cups of lemonade).

The woman yakked with Sue and Lauren for an hour before buying something.

Tom and Mary Ann, husband-and-wife neighbors who have an eight-month-old granddaughter, bought a kiddie slide and some children's ride-on vehicles.

"They've all been grandfather-tested," I assured them.

The sale ended at three p.m., at which time we calculated the day's receipts.

Lauren made a hundred and sixty dollars.

Sue made only thirty-two dollars.

"Considering the sale lasted for six hours," Lauren commented, "that's not even minimum wage."

Chloe and Lilly raked in a grand total of $6.25. I threw in ten bucks.

"Let's put it in our piggy banks!" Lilly said.

I got to take home the rest of the lemonade.

"Maybe," Chloe suggested, "you can have a lemonade stand at your house."

"The Pajama Game"

Every day, no matter what time I get up, I look like I just rolled out of bed. And nobody sees me, not even Sue, who either is still sleeping peacefully or is secretly awake and waiting for me to get up and make the coffee.

But on a recent morning, several astonished people saw my disheveled self because I ran errands in the pajamas I bought from my granddaughters' school fundraiser.

Chloe, who is in third grade, and Lilly, who is in kindergarten, were selling such fantastic and indispensable items as wrapping paper, which Sue bought, and nuts, which I am, so I shelled out (sorry) some money for a bag of them.

Also in the brochure were pajamas, which I had never seen when Lauren brought home school fundraisers.

She and Katie almost succeeded in bankrupting Sue and me with sales pitches for magazines, toys, games, and other things we didn't need or even want but bought anyway because we feared being known as the cheapest parents in town.

Instead, we ended up being the poorest.

When Katie and Lauren reached high school, they not only were still selling stuff but went to class every day wearing plaid flannel pajama bottoms, the hot style of the time.

Because the girls thought I was the most uncool man in America, I decided to prove them wrong. So one day, I wore pajamas to work.

Before I got there, however, Sue sent me out on some errands.

Everywhere I went — the bank, the post office, and the newsroom — flummoxed onlookers thought I was off my rocker. But Katie and Lauren, for the only time in their lives, said I was a dude of a dad.

The memories flooded what little remains of my mind when I saw the pajamas being sold in the fundraiser that Chloe and Lilly brought home.

I purchased a pair, which featured plaid bottoms with the school logo, and a blue, long-sleeved top, also with the school logo.

When they arrived, I put them on, hit the sack, and slept like a baby, or a log, or a grandfather who can no longer stay awake for the eleven o'clock news.

The next morning, I rolled out of bed — bright-tailed and bushy-eyed — and ran some errands.

My first stop was the gas station, where Chris, who manned the cash register, said my PJs were very stylish.

"They look comfy," he said, adding that he doesn't have kids and has never bought anything from a school fundraiser. "But you're not the only guy I have seen pumping gas in pajamas. A lot of people do it, mainly at night. But yours are definitely the nicest."

Next I went to the store to buy a birthday card for Sue and saw Christina, a shift manager who said, "You look good. I like the colors. You're very fashionable."

Christina said she has bought items from many school fundraisers.

"You can't say no," she told me.

"Have you ever bought pajamas?" I asked.

"Yes," Christina answered. "In fact, my husband wore fundraiser pajamas last night."

From there I went to the post office for a book of stamps and saw Renata, a friendly clerk who said, "You look good."

"Do I have your stamp of approval?" I wondered.

"Yes," replied Renata, who said she once bought pajamas from her daughter's school fundraiser. "They're hanging up. I don't wear them much — especially out in public."

My last stop was the bank, where a nice officer named Sharon said my pajamas looked terrific.

"When my daughter was in elementary school, I bought magazines, candy, and — my favorite — cookies," Sharon said. "There were sweatshirts in the fundraisers, but no pajamas. I like yours. And I like that you wore them to the bank. Your granddaughters will be proud of you."

When I got home, I told Sue about my PJ adventure.

"I got a lot of compliments," I reported. "And I didn't get arrested."

"That's always a good thing," she replied.

When I asked when the nuts would arrive, Sue looked at me and said, "The biggest one is already here."

"Hold the Phone, It's the Cops"

The call came in at 1:54 p.m.

"We are at the location," I reported. "Request backup."

"Who is this?" the police dispatcher asked.

It was me, plainclothes officer Jerry Zezima, star of the new real-life cop show "CSI: Columnist Stakeout Idiocy."

The premiere episode began a few nights before when my partner, Sue Zezima, who also happens to be my wife, lost her cellphone.

Thanks to some brilliant detective work, for which I must modestly take credit, it was determined that the item in question was stolen at the gym, where Sue had gone for the kind of rigorous training that not only cops must go through but also wives who routinely battle cumbersome vacuum cleaners, heavy soup pots, and, worst of all, lazy husbands.

After calling the service provider to disable the phone, which contained such valuable information as shopping coupons and photos of our grandchildren, we traced it to an address about half an hour away.

Our next move was to go to our local police precinct and report the theft.

"We put a trace on the phone," Sue told the desk sergeant.

"Where is it?" he asked.

When Sue gave him the location, the cop said, "Oh, shoot."

Except he didn't say "shoot."

"That's a rough neighborhood," he informed us.

"What should we do?" I asked.

"Go to the location," the desk sergeant said.

"I thought you said it was a rough neighborhood," I stammered.

"It is," he replied. "Go there, park down the street from the address, and call us. We'll send a car."

"Will there be any cops in the car?" I wondered.

"Yes," the sergeant assured me. "Good luck."

The next day, Sue and I got ready for our first stakeout.

I wore black, the preferred color of those in special operations. I just hoped I wouldn't need a special operation for gunshot wounds. I also wore shades, which didn't help much because it was raining.

Sue wore a gray hoodie.

"You're a girl in the hood," I said.

"And you're impossible," she responded.

"Copy that," I said before starting the motor of our unmarked vehicle. "Let's roll."

We drove to the location, parked a block away, and called the cops. Half an hour later, a car showed up. Officers Gallagher and O'Leary got out and walked over. I rolled down the window.

"What's going on?" Officer Gallagher inquired.

"We're here to nab a perpetrator," I responded.

"Huh?" Officer O'Leary said.

I explained the situation.

"It's our first stakeout," I said. "We're rookies."

"I can see that," said Officer Gallagher.

"This is my partner," I told the cops, pointing to Sue.

"And it was your phone that was stolen?" Officer O'Leary asked.

"Yes," Sue replied. "It's red."

"You were at the gym, right?" Officer O'Leary said.

"Yes," said Sue. "I was in a hurry to get home because I didn't want to miss 'Chicago Fire.'"

"Of course," I added with a wink, "our favorite is 'Chicago P.D.'"

"Of course," Officer O'Leary said.

"We're going to the address to check things out," Officer Gallagher said. "You stay here."

"10-4," I said.

The officers got back in their squad car, drove down the street, and parked in front of the house where the alleged thief resided. They knocked on the door, but I couldn't see what was happening.

"I hope they crack the case," I told Sue.

We waited for about fifteen minutes. Finally, the cops drove back to our car.

"Did you get the phone?" I asked.

"No," Officer Gallagher answered. "A nice couple lives there. They seemed like normal people. But we did scare the pants off them. The man even called his son, who wasn't home. The son said, 'Why would I go out of town to steal a phone?' There wasn't much more we could do."

"I guess this is now a cold case," I said.

"I guess so," said Officer O'Leary, who handed us a report.

"I'll call your precinct and put in a good word for you," I said. "Maybe you'll get a promotion to sergeant or admiral or something."

"Thanks," said Officer Gallagher, adding that he and Officer O'Leary see cases like ours every day.

"How come you don't have your own cop show?" I asked.

"It would be pretty boring," Officer Gallagher said.

With that, the men in blue drove away. Sue and I did the same.

The first and last episode of "CSI: Columnist Stakeout Idiocy" had come to an end.

"At least," I said with a shrug, "I didn't get arrested for impersonating an officer."

"Skate Expectations"

Because I have always thought that a double Axel is something in my car and that ice is best used in cocktails, I've never been a big fan of figure skating.

But now I can't get enough of it, especially after taking a lesson from two of the best figures in skating.

I refer to Chloe and Lilly, who had never skated before but managed to show me how to glide, slide, and land on my hide.

I hadn't been on ice skates since the Ice Age, which I am old enough to remember. That's why I was hoping to put on a mammoth performance for Chloe and Lilly, who begged me to take them skating when Sue and I were at an event sponsored by the Southold Mothers' Club, of which Lauren is a member.

While Lauren, a talented photographer, was on a photo shoot at the farm where the festivities were taking place, Sue and I watched Chloe and Lilly, who spent most of the afternoon outside with their friends, sipping hot chocolate and frolicking in bouncy houses — though not, of course, simultaneously.

As the day was winding down, the girls asked to go to the outdoor ice rink.

Sue said it was time to leave, so the girls turned to their old soft touch.

"Please, Poppie?" they pleaded.

Two minutes later, we were lacing on skates.

"This is the first time I have ever been ice skating!" Chloe told the attendant.

"Me, too!" Lilly chimed in.

"And you, sir?" the attendant asked me.

"I used to skate back in the day," I replied. "Unfortunately, the day was November 5, 1969."

"It's like riding a bike," he said.

"That means I won't forget how to fall on my keister," I assured him.

The rink wasn't quite like the one in Rockefeller Center, chiefly because it didn't have real ice.

"It's some sort of plastic that looks and feels like ice," the attendant explained. "But these are real ice skates."

The only one not wearing them was Sue, who was given a pair of foot covers that resembled shower caps and went over her sneakers.

As soon as I hit the ice, or whatever it was, the ice, or whatever it was, hit me.

Down I went. Luckily, I didn't land on my head, which would have broken the rink. Instead, I had to take the humiliation sitting down.

When I struggled to my feet, Chloe said, "Hold my hand, Poppie."

Lilly came over and held my other hand.

"We won't let you fall again," she promised.

The novices were giving the old-timer a lesson.

"Let's do a figure eight," I suggested.

"What's that?" Chloe asked.

When I explained the basic ice skating move, Lilly said, "We can do two figure eights."

"That would be a figure sixteen," said Chloe, who, unlike her grandfather, is a whiz at math.

Pushing my luck, I tried to do a camel spin, which sounds like a smelly form of desert transportation, and did a perfectly executed belly flop.

"Poppie, you need more practice," Chloe said sympathetically while helping me up.

As a hockey fan, I imagined I was lifting the Stanley Cup — with assistance from the girls, of course.

Then, because I somehow managed remain vertical, I recalled sportscaster Al Michaels's famous call when the United States shocked the Soviet Union in the 1980 Winter Olympics: "Do you believe in miracles? Yes!"

The girls and I spent the rest of the session performing moves that would have impressed Olympic judges if they had been members of the mothers' club.

I even danced with one of the plastic penguins that were supposed to aid shaky skaters like yours truly.

Finally, it was time to go.

"You did OK, Poppie," Chloe said as we took off our skates.

"For an old guy," Lilly added.

"Thank you, girls," I said. "I had fun, but my knees are a little sore."

"Maybe," Chloe said, "you should put some ice on them."

"Pillow Talk"

I am not a man to rest on my laurels, mainly because I don't have any. But I am a guy who can't help but rest on a burgeoning collection of popular items that are taking over not only the American home, but possibly the planet itself:

Pillows.

You can't go into any room in my house — except the bathroom, which could use something comfortable to sit on — without plopping on a packed pile of perfectly puffy pillows.

Thanks to Sue, the domestic diva here at the Zezimanse, there are, at last count, thirty-three pillows scattered about the premises.

A recent inventory revealed these startling numbers:

Seven on the bed in the master bedroom.

Six on the bed in another bedroom.

Two on the bed in a third bedroom.

Eight on the couch in the living room.

Two on a chair in the living room.

Six on the couch in the family room.

One on a chair in the family room.

One on another chair in the family room.

Grand total: thirty-three pillows.

There isn't a flat surface in the entire place — with the exception of my head — that isn't littered with pillows.

"Pillows make a house a home," Sue explained.

"If we had any more pillows," I said, "we'd need a second house to accommodate them all."

But it turns out that Sue and I don't have to apply for another mortgage because our good friends Hank and Angela Richert have even more pillows than we do.

"We're up to fifty-five," Angela told me over the phone.

"Hold on," Hank added. "I have to get a pillow off my head."

In what could become the Pillow Podcast, or an HGTV show called "Pillow Pals," we gave each other a FaceTime tour of our respective houses.

The first stop in Hank and Angela's beautiful home, which Sue and I haven't seen in person, was the master bedroom.

"We have eight pillows on the bed," Angela said.

"They breed like rabbits," Hank noted.

"Well," I pointed out, "they do spend a lot of time in bed."

"I'm still trying to train Hank to put them on the bed the right way," Angela said. "I made them to match the valances. The pillows have to be going the same way as the pattern on the valance. Hank puts them on the bed the wrong way."

"It's a pain when you go to bed at night because you have to take all the pillows off the bed," Hank said. "The question is: Where do you put them?"

"Baskets," Angela answered.

"We husbands will end up being basket cases," I said.

"We already are," said Hank.

"It's not just having pillows," Angela said. "It's how you dress your pillows. I have pillows dressed by season: spring, summer, fall, and winter. There also are holiday pillows for Thanksgiving and Christmas. And pillows with messages like, 'Nothing is more wonderful than family.' It's my mission to educate guys on pillow etiquette."

"I hope there's not a test," Hank said. "I'd flunk for sure."

"Hank refuses to fall in line," Angela said. "It's his way of protesting the pillows."

I must say that all the pillows in Hank and Angela's house are lovely, including those in the guest room.

"When you and Sue come to visit, that's where you'll stay," said Angela. "You can relax on the pillows."

"You can have some of ours, too," Hank said.

"This is what happens when you're retired," said Angela. "You get to argue about pillows."

There was no arguing that the Richerts have the Zezimas beat for pure pillow proficiency.

"This is our bed," I said while showing it on my phone camera. "We have only seven pillows."

"You're falling down on the job," Hank said.

"At least I'll land on a pillow," I responded.

The rest of the tour wasn't nearly as impressive as what I saw at Hank and Angela's house, which is a veritable pillow palace.

"You guys are the champs," I acknowledged.

"Thanks," said Hank. "But all this pillow talk is putting me to sleep."

"That's Using Your Shed"

If I had a sledgehammer, I'd sledgehammer in the morning, I'd sledgehammer in the evening, all over my land.

I won't sing the rest of it because: (a) the neighbors would call the cops and (b) I don't have a sledgehammer.

But I got to wield one when a crew of strong-armed guys came over to dismantle our old shed and put up a new one, where I keep all kinds of tools except — you guessed it — a screwdriver.

No, I mean a sledgehammer. I keep screwdrivers in the liquor cabinet.

Actually, I have gotten rid of so many tools, which are useless in my clumsy hands anyway, that I don't know why I even have a shed.

I used to have a lawn mower, a snow blower, and a power washer, but since I don't cut the grass, clear the driveway, or wash the house anymore, I dumped them on younger, more competent homeowners.

The rest of the shed was taken up by patio furniture, gardening supplies, and kiddie pools.

Tools included two rakes, a spade, a hoe, a trowel, a shovel, a pair of hedge clippers, and something that resembled a scythe. Whenever I used it to cut weeds, which grew back the next day, I looked like the Grim Geezer.

I also kept a hammock in the loft, but it was eaten by mice (the hammock, not the loft, though that was probably next).

In fact, the shed was in such deplorable condition that if I had sneezed on it, the whole rickety structure would have collapsed in a pile of kindling. So Sue and I decided to buy a new one.

We went to a place called Wood Kingdom and bought a shed made of, yes, wood. Unfortunately, it came unassembled.

"I am the least handy man in America," I told Maureen Schnapp, the owner. "I won't have to put it together myself, will I?"

"No," said Maureen, adding that the various parts — floor, walls, doors, roof, etc. — are made by an Amish company in Ohio.

"Will they deliver the materials by horse and buggy and have a shed-raising in my backyard?" I wondered.

"They're too busy for that," Maureen said. "They will get the parts to us. Then we'll send our guys over to tear down your old shed, cart it away, and put up the new one."

The guys were Jorge, forty-six, the supervisor, and his assistants, Juan, forty, and Jose, thirty-six.

When I saw Jose whacking the walls of the empty old shed with a sledgehammer, I walked up to him — being careful not to get hit in the head, in which case I'd have to buy the company a new sledgehammer — and asked, "May I try?"

"Sure," Jose replied. "But don't hurt yourself."

I grabbed the handle, lifted the sledgehammer with a jerk (me), and almost ruptured a vital organ.

"How much does this thing weigh?" I inquired.

"About forty pounds," Jose answered. "It's heavy."

"I'm old, but I'm strong," I assured him. "I keep in shape by bench-pressing six-packs."

Jose instructed me to stand inside the shed and hit the bottom of the Dutch roof, just above the top of the wall.

I reared back and slammed the metal hammerhead against the wood. Nothing.

"Try it again," Jose said.

I did. Still nothing. On my third swing, the wood began to crack.

"Nice," said Jose. "Keep going."

By this time, I was flailing away like one of the Property Brothers. I kept it up until the bottom of the roof had become separated from the wall. I also took a whack at one of the doors. I was amazed, not just at my terrific performance, but at the fact that I didn't go into cardiac arrest.

"You did a good job," said Jorge, who told me that he has a shed at home. "I keep tools in it. I also have the kids' pools. You can always use a shed. It's better than leaving stuff outside."

Thanks to the great work he, Jose, and Juan did, I don't have to leave stuff outside.

Now all my tools are inside a brand-new shed. I may even buy a sledgehammer. The Property Brothers will be impressed.

"Chime and Chime Again"

Since it's my job to ferret out problems, most of which I cause myself, I am obligated to report that my neighborhood is on high alert for a missing ferret.

That's the latest urgent message I have received from the company that operates the doorbell camera I recently purchased. It's especially unnerving considering that: (a) we don't have a doorbell and (b) the camera doesn't work.

But that hasn't stopped me from being inundated by daily alerts about Peeping Toms and weaselly critters that have been spotted near my house.

(For the record, ferrets aren't spotted, although some of them are striped. Stripes are what the Peeping Toms should be wearing. And a few of the reportedly missing cats that prowl my backyard are, I am sure, peeping toms.)

At any rate, this is alarming because the alarm company also sends me home security alerts so often that I now live in a constant state of home insecurity.

Then there's the neighborhood group that bombards me with emails about nefarious doings on my street.

I would become a shut-in except I'd keep receiving alerts about a motion being detected in the living room or a window being open in the kitchen.

It's a good thing the world can't see what goes on in the bathroom.

I wasn't about to tell a technician named Vinny, who came over to fix the alarm system.

"If you really want to feel safe, get a wireless camera," he advised. "You can install it yourself. A monkey could do it."

"Where can I rent one?" I asked.

"A camera?" Vinny said.

"No," I answered. "A monkey."

The next day, I went to a home improvement store and spoke with Tool Master Mike, who also is a camera guru.

"This is the kind you need," he said, handing me a small box containing an indoor-outdoor camera, batteries, a charger, and instructions that not even a monkey could understand.

"Will the camera pick up suspicious activity?" I wanted to know.

"Yes," Mike replied. "And suspicious characters."

"Like me?" I wondered.

"Could be," said Mike. "It also will detect dogs, bushes, leaves, and anything else that moves around. After a while, you will know if it's suspicious."

I took the camera home and instantly regretted not hiring an orangutan to put it up. The house's brick facade wasn't as much of an impediment as the fact that the stupid thing failed to function.

Technically, it operates fine, but since I decided to put it on a windowsill inside, it couldn't send moving images of what was going on outside.

I walked out the front door and waved to the camera, which miraculously didn't break when I flashed a dumb grin, but I might as well have been Claude Rains, who not only starred in the original screen version of "The Invisible Man" but also, for the time being, is dead.

Back inside, any movement in the living room set off a series of chimes that were so annoying, so relentless, so absolutely maddening that I wanted to smash the camera with a crowbar.

A friendly technician said over the phone that the camera couldn't pick up movement outside because the front window has two panes.

At that point, I had two pains — one in my head, the other in my neck.

"Put the camera outside and it will work," the technician said.

Fortunately, a great handyman named Andy, who was doing a job at the house with our equally great contractor, Anthony, put up a shelf on the window frame outside. When the guys return, they'll secure the security camera.

Then the chimes will start again. And all those other alerts will continue.

That's why I am on the lookout for a missing ferret. I hope it doesn't turn up in the bathroom.

"The Fab Floor"

This old man, he is dumb, he played knickknack with some rum.

The geezer in question is, naturally, yours truly. And I am floored to tell you that in order to get new flooring in the dining room and the living room of my house, I moved approximately one thousand three hundred and eighty-seven knickknacks, tchotchkes (I had to look up how to spell it), and, yes, bottles of booze from one room to another.

I would have swept it all under the rug except that we needed new rugs in both rooms to replace the magic carpets that were pulled up and left on the curb. The carpets magically disappeared when the garbage guys hauled them away.

Because a man's home is his hassle, I was required to help transfer all that stuff when Sue, the lady of the manor, in a manner of speaking, said she wanted new floors.

"Wouldn't new ceilings be easier?" I asked.

"No," Sue answered flatly. "We are going to get vinyl flooring."

"Is that your vinyl answer?" I wondered.

"Yes," she said. "Let's call Anthony."

That would be Anthony Amini, our contractor, who owns Performance Contracting and Management. He and his crew have done several great jobs at our house, including roofing and siding that would be the envy of any home improvement show.

Anthony's standout assistant is Andy Campanile, a handyman par excellence who does bricklaying, plumbing and, of course, flooring.

Before they started this daunting project — which included putting new floors in the front hallway and the adjacent half-bathroom, which was entirely redone and made me flush with excitement — Sue and I had to shop for new rugs.

"I'll take you out to lunch," she promised.

"I've been out to lunch for years," I replied.

"I know that," Sue said. "I mean, I'll buy you lunch if you come to the store with me."

It was a place that not only sells rugs, furniture, and all other kinds of household items, but also has a restaurant that serves, among other offerings, Swedish meatballs.

Stuffed more than the seat cushion of my favorite easy chair, I staggered through the aisles as Sue looked for the perfect covering to lay down in the dining room.

When she had settled on a rug, I asked if I could settle on the rug to take a nap.

"No!" she exclaimed, strongly implying that I was, indeed, out to lunch.

Then came the hard part: Bringing almost everything in the dining room to the living room so Anthony and Andy could install a new floor. That meant emptying the liquor cabinet, which contained the aforementioned rum, as well as whiskey, gin, vodka, and so many other spirits that they could have anesthetized an army.

We also had to clean out the hutch, which contained glasses, china, and silverware that, if put on a scale, would have weighed more than a pregnant walrus.

As I labored to cart stuff into the living room, I was hunched over like the Hutch-back of Notre Dumb.

When the dining room was finished, we had to reverse the process: Bring everything back to the dining room and also bring everything from the living room to the dining room so Anthony and Andy could put down a new floor in the living room.

It was a room with a whew.

The items included Hummels, lamps, and enough books to fill a wing of the New York Public Library.

When Anthony and Andy had put down the new floor, Sue and I had to — you guessed it! — transfer everything back to the living room.

I must say that the flooring looks great, Anthony and Andy did another terrific job, and Sue is thrilled.

As for me, this old man can't wait to sit down, take a deep breath, and play knickknack with some rum.

"The Dance of the Dunce"

If I were in a dancing competition, I would never experience the thrill of victory, but I sure would know the agony of the feet.

Unless, of course, the judge took pity on me.

That's exactly what happened when I found myself in a dance-off with Chloe and Lilly.

The girls are veritable pros compared to me, a geezer with the smooth moves and fancy footwork of a drunken platypus. Forget hip-hop. My specialty would be hip-replacement-hop.

This was sadly evident when Chloe and Lilly challenged me to a dance-off in which I almost needed CPR (Clumsy Poppie Resuscitation).

The judge was Sue, who wisely sat this one out.

It was the culmination of a wonderful day that began when the girls were in a recital sponsored by Inspire Dance Centre, where they take lessons.

Last summer, they were in an outdoor show at a vineyard, where Sue and I toasted the dancing stars with glasses of vintage grapes. This time, the "Winter Showcase" was held in a roller skating rink.

And the girls were, indeed, on a roll, even though they wore dancing shoes instead of skates. They were each in only one routine in the twenty-dance program, but they performed so well, in my humble and totally unbiased opinion, that if they were on "Dancing With the Stars," hard-marking judge Len Goodman would have given them perfect scores.

I certainly did when Lilly stole the show in a dance from "Cinderella" and Chloe did the same in a routine performed to the Meghan Trainor song "Better When I'm Dancin'."

When Lilly came out with the other girls in her group, she stood in the front row, stage right, though to me it looked like stage left, which is one of the many reasons, chief of which is a complete lack of performing talent, why I am not on Broadway.

As the music played, Lilly moved her arms in a wavy motion, then swayed to the beat, raised her hands above her head, sang a line of the song, did a pirouette, moved to the back, spun clockwise, and exited with the others. She was the last one off and got a huge ovation.

"That was adorable!" Sue exclaimed.

Naturally, I agreed.

We had the same reaction for the next number, which featured Chloe. It was an upbeat performance in which she and the other girls in her group danced, pranced, and clapped. Chloe had perfect timing. At the song's conclusion, she and her fellow dancers knelt at the front of the stage and got a big round of applause. The loudest ovation was, of course, for Chloe.

When the show was over, Lauren and Guillaume beamed with pride through the face masks everyone was required to wear.

Sue and I presented Chloe and Lilly with flowers.

"They smell!" Lilly said.

"That may not prevent her from eating them," remarked Lauren, noting that Lilly has a big appetite for such a little girl. Elton John's "Tiny Dancer" could have been written about her.

When we got back to Lauren and Guillaume's house, Chloe and Lilly challenged me to a dance-off.

"Nini," Chloe said to Sue, "you can be the judge."

Lilly got her FreeTime and started playing "Gold Digger," a Billboard hit from Ye, the artist formerly known as Kayne West.

We all started jumping around. Chloe and Lilly did handstands. I waved my hands, stamped my feet, and almost keeled over.

"Freeze!" Lilly shouted as she turned off the song.

Sue deliberated for a moment and announced, "Lilly wins."

When the song began again, the girls went into even greater gyrations. I gasped for air as I tried to emulate their moves.

"Freeze!" Lilly shouted.

The song stopped and Sue said, "Chloe wins."

But the third time was the charm. I danced up a storm, putting my right index finger on the top of my head and spinning like a top.

It was, literally, a dizzying performance that not only impressed the judge but had her in stitches.

"Poppie wins," Sue declared.

I could tell she took pity on me, but for a man with two left feet, which makes shoe shopping difficult, it made a great day even better.

I didn't get flowers, like Chloe and Lilly, but I felt like a dancing star.

"Thanks," I said to Sue. "You're a much better judge than Len Goodman."

"Portrait of the Artist as a Family Guy"

As a husband, father, and grandfather, which puts me at the bottom of the family pecking order, I have a lot in common with Brian Crane, the Reuben Award-winning cartoonist who created the wildly popular syndicated comic strip "Pickles."

The only real difference between us — aside from the incredible fact that he has sixteen more grandchildren than I do — is that I'm such a bad artist, I couldn't even draw a good salary.

"My grandkids are van Gogh compared to me," I told Brian in a phone chat. "Except they still have all their ears."

"Maybe they can start a comic strip," Brian suggested.

"It could be about a grandfather with a mustache," I said. "He'd be the butt of the jokes."

"Hey, that sounds familiar," Brian said.

No wonder. The star of "Pickles" is Earl, a mustachioed grandfather who, more often than not, is the butt of the jokes in the family, which includes his loving but long-suffering wife, Opal. The retired couple live with their daughter, Sylvia; grandson, Nelson; dog, Roscoe; and cat, Muffin.

My loving but long-suffering wife, Sue, is a big fan of the strip. So is yours truly, a mustachioed grandfather who, more often than not, is the butt of the jokes in the family, which includes two daughters and five grandchildren.

Brian has a loving but long-suffering wife of his own, Diana, with whom he will celebrate fifty years of marriage in June.

"Sue and I will celebrate our forty-fourth anniversary on April 2," I informed Brian.

"What a coincidence!" he said. "April 2 is when 'Pickles' debuted in 1990."

"I wanted to get married on April Fools' Day," I said, "but Sue nixed the idea because she was afraid I would get her whoopee cushions as anniversary gifts."

Another thing Brian and I have in common is that we are January babies: He was born on the third, I arrived on the eleventh.

"The only famous person who was born on my birthday was Alexander Hamilton," I said. "That means I'll either have a hit Broadway show or be killed in a duel."

"I don't know of anyone famous who was born on my birthday," said Brian, who is seventy-three and, though five years older than I am, is a fellow baby boomer.

"My due date was December 20," I told him. "I was born more than three weeks later and haven't been on time for anything since."

"Your mother should have sent you an eviction notice," said Brian, adding: "I was due in December, too. I was a breech birth. I came out feet first."

"I landed on my head," I said. "It explains a lot."

Mining humor from family situations is also a similarity — except Brian's clan is a lot larger than mine. He has seven children and twenty-one grandchildren.

"How do you keep track of them all?" I wondered.

"That's a good question for my wife," said Brian. "Our oldest child is a son in his forties and our youngest is a daughter in her twenties somewhere. It keeps changing all the time. My wife has the ability to figure it out. It's like a miracle to me. But I do know all their names."

Then there are the grandchildren.

"We have a bunch of them," Brian said. "It's quite a dynasty. My wife knows their ages, weights, sizes, everything. I can recognize them on sight. The oldest is a sophomore in college. The youngest two were born a year ago. They're not twins; they're cousins who are a month apart."

"Do you know all their names, too?" I asked.

"Yes," Brian replied proudly. "Although sometimes things get so crazy, I can't remember my own name."

If so, Diana will be there to help.

"She's always been there for me," said Brian, adding that Diana encouraged him when he told her about his "secret ambition" to do a comic strip. "I was working for an advertising agency. I was in my late thirties and we were accumulating more children. I didn't know how we could afford it. But she said, 'You have to do it.' I said, 'I don't have the talent.' I was rejected by three syndicates, but Diana wouldn't let it go. I wouldn't be doing this if it weren't for her. She's my first editor and biggest supporter."

Now, more than thirty years later, "Pickles" is syndicated by the Washington Post Writers Group in more than nine hundred newspapers. Brian also has produced nine "Pickles" books.

"How much of Earl is you and how much of Opal is Diana?" I asked.

"Roughly, I'm Earl and she's Opal, but there are days when I'm Opal and she's Earl," Brian said. "We do display both characteristics. She's more outgoing. I'm an introvert. In a crowd, I clam up. She does all the talking. Also, I'm not very handy. My father-in-law was the world's best mechanic. My wife expected I would be like that. She was greatly disappointed. She's pretty handy. She can do things I wouldn't try. And she's smarter than I am. She can figure things out better than I can."

"My wife is the same way," I said. "And, like Opal, she's married to a guy with a mustache."

"You look good in a mustache," said Brian. "I, on the other hand, look ridiculous. I grew one and my wife said, 'Shave that silly thing off.' A few years ago I had Earl shave his mustache. Then I came up with the idea to have readers vote to bring it back or not. I put out a call for entries. I even had a post office box. You wouldn't believe the amount of mail I got. They voted for Earl to keep his mustache."

"My grandchildren would vote for me to keep my mustache, too," I said.

"They could put that in their comic strip," Brian suggested.

"Maybe it'll be syndicated," I said. "They can call it 'Poppie,' which is what they call me."

"Will you be the butt of the jokes?" Brian asked.

"Of course," I said. "And like any good grandfather, I know all the kids' names."

"A Grave Situation"

If I have learned anything in my nearly seven decades on this globe — aside from the fact that life is too short for light beer — it is this:

The older you get, the younger old people seem to be.

This was driven home (though not, thank God, in hearse) when three things happened.

(a) Sue and I redid our wills.

(b) I got a brochure in the mail from a cemetery.

(c) My doctor said I won't have to worry about the first two for a long time, although he did add that for enough money, he could have me declared legally dead.

All of these comforting thoughts entered what little remains of my mind when Sue and I visited our lawyer, Tim Danowski.

"Are you going to discuss our habeas corpses?" I asked.

"That's a dead issue," said Tim, who drew up what he called "I love you" wills.

First we went over Sue's will, which refers to me, in Article IV, as her "beloved husband."

"I notice that in Article V, I am not 'beloved' anymore," I pointed out. "I'm just referred to as Sue's husband."

I didn't worry about it because the "beloved" reference to Sue, and subsequent lack thereof, was the same in my will, which also detailed what would happen if I became incoherent.

"My family thinks I'm that way now," I said.

Then we got down to assets and what our children would get.

"We don't have millions of dollars," Sue said.

"We have dozens of dollars," I added.

"Our younger daughter has already said she wants my ice cream," Sue told Tim.

"All I have of any value are beer, wine, and Three Stooges memorabilia," I said. "Let the kids fight over it."

"They won't have to do it for quite a while," said Tim. "You guys are young."

"When you get to be our age," I told Tim, who is in his thirties, "anyone who is older is young. Even if a guy dies when he's eighty, we'll say, 'What a shame. Cut down in the prime of life.' Now that we aren't young anymore, nobody else is old."

"That's one way to look at it," said Tim, whom we thanked for his excellent work in helping us get our affairs in order.

And not a moment too soon because the very next day, I got a brochure from Pinelawn Memorial Park and Arboretum.

"Give your loved ones a gift that will provide peace of mind and lasting comfort," it read. "Those who visit Pinelawn Memorial Park and Arboretum will find themselves surrounded in the beauty of the grounds with wide-sweeping lawns that feature majestic trees, colorful flower beds, historic sculptures, and tranquil fountains. This carefully planned and expertly maintained landscape has made Pinelawn the most beautiful memorial park in America."

"All I have to do," I told Sue, "is die."

"I'll visit you once a week," she promised.

I wanted a second opinion. So I saw my physician, Dr. Antoun Mitromaras.

"Tell the people at the cemetery to call me," Dr. Mitromaras said. "I'll tell them that I won't let you die."

"Do I have a pulse?" I asked the good doctor.

"Yes," he announced, adding that my blood pressure was perfect and my weight was normal.

"I guess the cemetery will have to wait to get business from me," I said.

"Unless they want to give me ten thousand dollars," Dr. Mitromaras said. "Then I can arrange for you to be a customer."

My heart raced.

"Just kidding," said Dr. Mitromaras, an eighty-year-old jokester who knows that laughter is the best medicine.

"What's your secret of longevity?" I asked.

"Minerals," he responded.

"Aren't they hard to swallow?" I wondered.

"Not if they're in pill form," Dr. Mitromaras said. "Multivitamins are good, too. So is physical activity. And nuts."

"I'm nuts," I informed him.

"I know," he said, adding that when he dies, he wants an above-ground tomb. "In case I wake up in a year or two. And I want it with a glass ceiling and a view of the water."

"You want a tomb with a view?" I asked.

"It's the only way to go," said Dr. Mitromaras.

When I got home, I told Sue that I passed my physical with flying colors.

"It looks like you're stuck with your 'beloved' husband," I said. "And now I can tell the people at the cemetery to drop dead."

CHAPTER 10

(For baby boomers, reminiscing is the sport of champions. Looking ahead — even with prescription eyewear — can be enlightening, too. But there also are obstacles to overcome. And more adventures to enjoy.)

"High School Reunion: The Big 5-Oh!"

There is a saying among people of a certain age that we're like fine wine: We're not getting older, we're getting better.

This adage was proven beyond a reasonable doubt — even though there is doubt that I have ever been reasonable — at my fiftieth high school reunion, where I drank some mighty fine wine and Sue won two bottles of the stuff.

Sue and I attended Stamford Catholic High School, Class of 1971, where Sue was the epitome of class and I was the class clown.

So when it came time to get together with fellow classmates to mark half a century since we graduated, we headed to our hometown of Stamford, Connecticut, for a weekend of fun, frolic, and — with apologies to Marcel Proust, an author I was supposed to read in high school but never did — remembrance of things past.

The reunion committee, headed by Vivian Vitale, did a tremendous job of coordinating the event, which drew about a hundred people. They included Hank Richert, who was my college roommate for three years and was the best man at my wedding to Sue, as I was at Hank's wedding to his wife, Angela, who didn't go to Catholic High but, as Hank's guest, added wit and elegance to the proceedings. They are dear friends we hadn't seen in a long time.

Needless to say, but I'll say it anyway, Sue and Angela looked beautiful. Hank and I looked almost respectable. Everyone else looked good, too. And this wasn't astigmatism talking. Or even the wine.

"It's a shame that our kids are getting older but we're not," I told one classmate. "I feel sorry for them, but what are you going to do?"

The reason I couldn't identify him was that, at first, I didn't know who he was. That's because, the evening before the reunion, we attended a meet-and-greet at Zody's 19th Hole, a great restaurant where, unfortunately, there were no name tags for us to identify other attendees.

"You don't know who I am," a second guy said to me.

"Do you know who you are?" I asked.

"Yes," he replied.

"Prove it," I said.

He pulled out his wallet and showed me his police badge (he's a retired cop), which had his name.

"You're Bob Shawinsky," I told him.

"That's right!" he said.

"See?" I announced triumphantly. "I do know who you are."

I'm lucky he didn't arrest me. But we did have some laughs, a sure sign of our arrested development.

Another guy, Don Sabia, gave me his business card, which contained his alleged occupation: "Consigliere."

I kissed his ring.

It was a fantastic evening, but the best was yet to come.

The following night, we had the reunion at the Stamford Yacht Club, which went all out for us with dining, dancing, and, yes, name tags.

"Zez!" more than one person exclaimed, using my most popular nickname (and the only one that can be repeated here). "What have you been up to?"

"No good," I replied each time.

It didn't surprise anybody because, fifty years ago, I spent so much time in the principal's office that the administration could have charged me rent.

"I was on the dishonor roll," I told a classmate.

"You graduated anyway," she pointed out.

"They couldn't wait to get rid of me," I said.

"You look great," another classmate said. "What's your secret?"

"Spackle," I replied. "It hides the wrinkles."

Bridget Ormond Kopek, who was on the reunion committee, announced that we were going to have an "organ recital" before the formal festivities.

"You can discuss your organs, backs, eyes, and any other medical problems," she explained.

One guy called himself the "bionic man" because he has had knee and hip replacements and lots of other surgeries.

"There isn't too much of the original me left," he said.

Another classmate complained of constant soreness.

"What do you do for joint trouble?" he asked.

"Move to a new joint," I suggested.

Many of the conversations centered on grandchildren. Sue and I have five — the most, as far as I know, of anyone there.

"And," I told a group standing next to the bar, "they're all more mature than I am."

Retirement also was a big topic of conversation.

"I don't know how I could have stopped working when I never really started," I said to a couple of classmates.

"Do you get in your wife's hair?" I was asked.

"Yes," I responded. "Shampoo doesn't help."

After dinner, it was time to hit the dance floor.

"Do you have your dancing shoes on?" a woman asked.

"I sure do," I said. "And they still fit my two left feet."

Sue and I boogied to "My Girl," which was appropriate because she has been mine for forty-three years.

"You missed our wedding song," Sue said, referring to "Can't Help Falling in Love."

"Sorry," I said. "I was in the bathroom swapping funny stories with a few of the guys."

We stayed out on the floor for several more oldies until the raffle, which was held to defray expenses.

Among the items on the list were three copies of my latest book, "Every Day Is Saturday."

"I'll sign them," I promised, "which will reduce their value even more."

The most coveted items were bottles of wine.

When the number on one of Sue's tickets was called, she shrieked, "That's me! I won! I never win anything!"

Lightning — actually, cabernet — struck twice when Sue won again.

"This is your lucky night," I told her.

It was a lucky night for everyone because the reunion couldn't have been better.

To all our classmates of fifty years, a toast of wine and rousing cheers!

"The Heart of the Matter"

Love means never having to say you're sorry for not doing the laundry.

For the first time in forty-three years of marriage, I have been washing clothes. I've also been performing tasks I did before but am now doing more frequently, like loading the dishwasher, vacuuming the house, cleaning the bathrooms, going grocery shopping, and playing chauffeur.

There's a good reason for this uncharacteristic usefulness: Sue had a heart attack.

She's recovering slowly but well. She gets tired easily, especially after watching me fold the clothes I just took out of the dryer and pile them on the bench in the family room. And she will be the first to say that this life-changing event came as a shock — though not, in retrospect, as a surprise.

"The warning signs were there for months," Sue admitted. "I chose to ignore them."

She's not unlike a lot of people who shrug off chest discomfort as stress or indigestion (in our house, I'm the cause of both). This is especially true of men and women of a certain age (in Sue's case, sixty-eight) who acknowledge that they're no longer spring chickens but don't think they are old enough to have a heart attack.

Sue also wasn't a good candidate for cardiac problems because she's slim, she exercises daily, she eats healthily, and she doesn't have either high blood pressure or high cholesterol.

But she does have a family history of heart issues. And that, even without the warning signs, should have been a warning sign.

The attack happened the day after Thanksgiving, at Lauren's house. It was late morning and Sue and I were preparing to go home after what Chloe and Lilly called "a double sleepover" (we spent Wednesday and Thursday nights there).

I loaded the car while Sue was in the bathroom. Right after I came back in, she emerged ashen-faced and said she had just vomited. She sat down and said she was having chest pains that radiated to her back. She also felt dizzy.

Lauren, who is on the ball with everything, said Sue needed to go to the hospital. I concurred. I probably should have called an ambulance, but the hospital was close by, so I drove Sue to the emergency room.

Her EKG was normal, but her blood work showed an elevated enzyme level, a sure sign of a heart attack.

Sue was rushed into surgery. Two hours later, Dr. Andrew Persits came out and told me that Sue had an attack during the procedure.

"I did an angiogram," he said. "Two or three spots in her left anterior descending artery were seventy to eighty percent blocked, so I put in three stents. Her right side was forty to fifty percent blocked, but that can be managed with medication."

Sue stayed in the hospital for two nights and was released on Sunday morning.

Dr. Persits and all the other doctors, nurses, and technicians who attended to Sue at Peconic Bay Medical Center in Riverhead, New York, were wonderful. In fact, they were lifesavers — wintergreen, the best kind.

When Sue got home, it was my turn to attend to her. Even for a writer, words can't adequately express the depth of my love for her. That's why I was happy to be the caregiver for someone whose care and giving have made her the backbone of our family.

Which brings me to the laundry.

"I appreciate that you're doing it," said Sue, who had to show me how to use the washer and dryer. "But you think you do it the best. You hadn't done it for forty-three years, but now that you've been doing it for a week, you think you're the King of Laundry."

"I do a pretty good job," I said immodestly. "And I haven't flooded the house."

"Even though you know how to do the laundry, you don't know how to put it away," Sue responded. "You just let it pile up. It's clean, but it's in piles."

She did have kind words for my ability to do other household chores.

"You do clean the bathrooms. And you vacuum nicely. It gets me off the hook," Sue said. "You also do a good job with the dishes. I can tell because you have dishpan hands."

Before dinner, I set the table. And I clear it off afterward. But if it were left to me to prepare meals, we both would starve.

"You don't cook," Sue reminded me. "You don't know how to turn on the oven and you don't turn the stove off."

That's not entirely true because, by Sue's admission, I do make scrambled eggs. I also heat up leftover pizza in the oven. And I can operate the microwave.

"At least I haven't burned the house down," I said in my own feeble defense.

Sue said she's grateful that I chauffeur her around, mainly to go to doctor's appointments and to run errands. Because she's not yet ready to get behind the wheel, I am the designated driver — even though I don't have a chauffeur's cap.

"You've been very good about it," Sue said sweetly. "But," she added, "I don't like going to the grocery store with you. You're always ten paces behind me. Then you wander off somewhere. And you put stuff in the cart that we don't need."

"We always need beer," I countered.

Sue smiled, took one of my dishpan hands, and said, "Thank you for taking such good care of me."

"It's my pleasure," I responded with a kiss.

"I know being a caregiver isn't easy," she said.

"It's easier than being a patient," I said.

"I'm getting better every day," Sue said. "Some days I get tired, but overall, I'm doing all right. I just never thought this would happen to me."

"Once you start cardio rehab, you'll be back to normal," I assured her. "And I did buy that pillbox for you."

"You mean the old lady pillbox," Sue said with a smile. "I went from not taking anything to taking five pills a day."

"Am I a pill?" I asked.

Sue smiled again and said, "No. You're good medicine."

We both laughed because laughter is the best medicine — and the cheapest.

"Now if you will excuse me," I said, "I have to do another load of laundry."

"The Zezima Family Christmas Letter"

Since I am in the holiday spirit (and, having just consumed a mug of hot toddy, a glass of eggnog, and a nip of cheer, the holiday spirits are in me), I have decided to follow in that great tradition of boring everyone silly by writing a Christmas letter.

That is why I am pleased as punch (which I also drank) to present the following chronicle of the Zezima family, which includes Jerry, the patriarch; Sue, the matriarch; Katie and Lauren, the daughtersiarch; Dave and Guillaume, the sons-in-lawiarch; and Chloe, Lilly, Xavier, Zoe, and Quinn, the grandchildreniarch.

Dear friends:

It sure has been an eventful year for the Zezimas!

The family got a shot in the arm by getting shots in the arm. It wasn't so easy for Jerry and Sue because they couldn't schedule an appointment for their first vaccinations, so Katie and Lauren, who are a tad more tech savvy than their parents, went online and made appointments for them.

At the suggestion of college buddy and fellow father Tim Lovelette, who said, "That's why God gave us kids — to keep us alive," Jerry tried to get a shot and a beer. Unfortunately, the bar was closed.

But Jerry and Sue did get both rounds of the vaccine, plus a later booster, which encouraged Jerry to needle everyone else. When he told Olivia, the nice medical technician who gave him his second shot, that now the public wouldn't be safe from his stupid jokes, she said, "People may have to be vaccinated against you."

This newfound freedom, after many months of quarantine, enabled Jerry and Sue to have family reunions. One of the best occurred when they drove to Washington, D.C., to visit Katie, Dave, Xavier, Zoe, and Quinn, whom they hadn't seen in a year and a half.

They went to the zoo (surprisingly, Jerry wasn't put on exhibit with the other monkeys), had fun at a kiddie birthday party (it wasn't for Jerry), watched Zoe and Quinn's soccer practice (Jerry got a kick out of it), took Xavier to a baseball game (Jerry had a ball but didn't catch one), saw the sights (Jerry wasn't one of them), and generally had a grand time (because Jerry and Sue are grandparents).

As they were leaving, Katie told Jerry that Zoe and Quinn, who were infants during the previous visit, had joined the other grandkids in "The Cult of Poppie."

Jerry and Sue also got to see a lot more of Chloe and Lilly, who live nearby but whom they had seen in person only periodically, and then it had to be outdoors while masked and at a safe social distance.

Now they could hug, kiss, and, in Jerry's case, act silly.

Among the highlights:

A spirited game of Wiffle ball, in which Chloe and Lilly hit home runs but mighty Poppie struck out.

A dance recital at a vineyard, where Jerry and Sue celebrated Chloe and Lilly's dazzling performances with wine.

A beauty session in which Lilly painted Jerry's fingernails pink and purple (Sue and Lauren were aghast, but Jerry explained that sometimes a boy just likes to feel pretty).

And a yard sale where Jerry helped Chloe and Lilly with a lemonade stand that netted a grand total of $6.25.

At another family reunion, Jerry visited his mother, Rosina, for the first time in fifteen months. Mom, now ninety-seven and sharper than her son, which admittedly isn't saying much, reminded Jerry that their time apart was even longer than the ten months she was pregnant with him.

"But," Mom said sweetly, "it was worth the wait."

A few weeks later, she visited Jerry and Sue with Jerry's sisters, Elizabeth and Susan. Lauren and Guillaume were there, too, as were Chloe and Lilly, who lovingly call their great-grandmother Gigi.

On the domestic front, Jerry and Sue had new siding put on the outside of their house and new flooring inside — which, Jerry stupidly pointed out, was better than the other way around. Jerry also helped a bricklayer repair a crack in the foundation, which was not as hard as Jerry's head.

The Zezimas got a new shed to replace the old one, which was home to a family of mice that ate Jerry's hammock. Jerry got revenge by using a sledgehammer to help knock down the dilapidated structure.

In the field of entertainment, Jerry tried out to be a contestant on "Wheel of Fortune," but he never got a chance to meet Pat and Vanna — or win any money — because he was far from letter perfect.

In crime news, Sue's cellphone was stolen. In cooperation with the local police department, she and Jerry went on a stakeout that didn't produce the phone but could have served as the pilot episode for a cop show called "CSI: Columnist Stakeout Idiocy."

The biggest event of the year was Jerry and Sue's fiftieth high school reunion. They had a blast, especially because they got to be with their good friends Hank and Angela Richert, whom they hadn't seen in several years. It was unanimously agreed that everyone looked great and that Jerry was still the class clown.

In good health news, Jerry joined a gym. He told a personal trainer that his main form of exercise is doing twelve-ounce curls. The trainer said it was a unique way to work out, which gave Jerry a great excuse to stay home and drink beer.

In bad health news, Sue had a heart attack. Jerry drove her to the hospital, where she had three stents put in her left artery. It was a scare, to be sure, but Sue is feeling much better and is on the road to recovery. Jerry has taken the role of caregiver and has actually done laundry for the first time in forty-three years of marriage. Love conquers all!

We hope you and your family have also overcome the challenges of this difficult year and have had fun in the process.

Merry Christmas with love, laughter, and gratitude from the Zezimas.

EPILOGUE

On a post in the finished basement of my mother's house, where she has been living since the Johnson administration (Lyndon, not Andrew), is a plaque that reads: "Never regret growing old. It's a privilege denied to many."

It sums up Mom's outlook on life.

Mine, too.

It's now Sue's as well. Ever since her heart attack, she has been appreciating things a bit more. Not that she didn't before, but she's a dynamo who has always put others first.

"A person's best friend is a clear conscience," I told her. "You're not selfish, so you shouldn't feel guilty about thinking of yourself once in a while."

Sue nodded in agreement. Still, age was on her mind.

"I remember turning thirty — and I thought that was old," she said. "Where does the time go?"

"One of two places," I responded. "The Federal Witness Protection Program or the Caribbean. And it doesn't even have the courtesy to send us postcards."

I embrace getting older. It's not really so bad. And it beats the alternative.

Sue knows and appreciates this. So does my mother.

On a recent visit, I took Mom for her weekly appointment with her hairdresser, Ronnie Fowler, who has been making my mother look younger and even more beautiful for more than half a century.

"I'll never forget the time your mother was in the hospital. As she was being wheeled into the operating room for emergency surgery, she said,

'Call Ronnie to cancel my appointment for tomorrow!'" Ronnie said with a laugh.

My mother, who had just gotten her snowy strands shampooed and styled, confirmed the story.

"I didn't want Ronnie to wonder why I didn't come in," my mother said with a laugh of her own.

Ronnie, an astonishingly youthful-looking seventy-one, has been a tonsorial artist for fifty-three years. My mother has been going to her for all but one of those years.

"She's my oldest customer," said Ronnie, who used to have her own salon, Ronnie's Best Little Hair House, but now rents a chair at a nearby establishment in Stamford called Flor Hair & Style.

"I cut your father's hair, too," Ronnie continued. "He was a sweet man."

She reminded me that she also cut Sue's hair. As kids, Katie and Lauren went to Ronnie as well. My sisters, Elizabeth and Susan, still do. And when they were young, Susan's now-grown children, Taylor, Blair, and Whitney, also went to her.

"I did the whole family — except you," Ronnie said to me. "You're the one who got away."

"You'd need a hedge trimmer for my hair," I said, adding that I used to look like the late rock legend Billy Preston, who was famous for his enormous Afro.

"In the seventies and eighties, all you guys did," Ronnie remarked. "Guys with straight hair would come in to get perms."

My mother, said Ronnie, has hair that is "pin straight," necessitating a perm every three months.

When I told Ronnie about my barber on Long Island, Maria Santos, she said, "Maria does a great job. She makes you look younger."

"And you make my mother look younger," I said as Mom and I were about to leave.

"That's what I love to do," said Ronnie. "The key is to feel and act younger, too."

As I like to say to anybody who will listen, which narrows the field considerably, "Never grow up and you will never grow old."

That's the problem with a lot of grown-ups: They have grown up — and old — before their time.

One of the worst things that can befall an adult is to forget what it was like to be a child.

"Do you spoil your grandchildren?" I am frequently asked.

My patented response: "No. That's my wife's job. My job is to corrupt them."

That's why they love to play with me. And I with them.

The body may be sore the next day, but the mind is still running around and being silly.

When you get to be a certain age, that same mind turns to what your legacy will be. Some people are concerned about leaving material wealth to their children and grandchildren. Others try to atone for past mistakes and make everything right before the inevitable happens.

No matter what your station in life is, no matter what your personal situation is, whether longevity runs in your family, as it does in mine, or if time appears to be short, I think you should do what a child would do, something that would, in a small but not insignificant way, be the best legacy of all:

Fill the world with love and laughter, and make it a better place.

Printed in the United States
by Baker & Taylor Publisher Services